THE OFFICIAL

BATTLESTAR
GALACTICA ™*

SCRAPBOOK

THE OFFICIAL
BATTLESTAR
GALACTICA™
SCRAPBOOK

by
James Neyland

Publishers · GROSSET & DUNLAP · New York
A FILMWAYS COMPANY

Thanks to Richard James, Mary Welch, David Klassen, Corinne DeLucca, Bonnie Mendelsohn, and Martha Urann.

Designed by Marcia Ben-Eli

To Douglas and Laura

CONTENTS

PROLOGUE

There are those who believe that life here began out there, far across the universe, with tribes of humans who may have been the forefathers of the Egyptians, or the Toltecs, or the Mayans. Some believe that there may yet be brothers of man who, even now, fight to survive, somewhere beyond the heavens.

THE STATE OF THE GALAXY

Somewhere in the universe, an enormous craft leads a motley convoy through the galaxies. The passengers search for a planet only dimly recalled in their history, a planet that may or may not exist. For these space-travelers, who are known as humans, the existence of this lost civilization offers the only hope of survival.

All they know is that this planet they seek is called "Earth."

On Earth, possibly millions of miles away, other humans sit in front of television screens watching the travails of these travelers, aware

Standing beside their star chart, the three leading Colonial Warriors, Apollo, Starbuck, and Boomer, discuss a matter of strategy.

of the vast distance separating them in space, but unsure of the distance in time. They are tantalized by the existence of this culture so much like their own, yet credibly different; they want to know who these people are and how they are related to life on Earth. Are they the ancestors who colonized Earth millennia ago, building the Pyramids and Stonehenge? Are they the descendants of Twentieth-Earth-Century humankind seeking to return millennia hence? Or do they exist in the same time frame, out there in space now, seeking to land at any moment?

These are questions that cannot be answered, questions that give the events observed a great urgency.

By A.D. 1978, in the twenty-first year of their own space explorations, Earth humans have become aware of the limitations of their recorded history. They are aware that some of their kind may exist on other planets, in other galaxies, though they are unsure and frightened by questions of what these other peoples may be like.

On the screens they view, the Earth humans have seen a society much like their own, one that is both reassuring and unsettling—reassuring, because these space humans, called the Colonials, share the same innate good qualities of Earth humans; unsettling, because they also share the same weaknesses and evils. The problems the Colonials face are timeless, eternal problems, and viewing them reveals much about the human condition wherever or whenever humans exist.

Whether in space or on Earth, humans face a continuing conflict between a passion for freedom and a compulsion for order and control. Within their species, a wide range of personality and behavior is possible—from the wise, mature, and responsible individual to the selfish, venal, greedy, and ruthless. Such extremes of individuality constitute both the greatest blessing and the most plaguing curse of humankind. Witnessing the struggle in space, Earth humans are able to reflect upon similar problems they have faced on their own planet. And this reflection is important to them

in the eighth decade of their twentieth century, for many of them have lost the ability to see their own struggles with clarity.

The largest of the spacecraft that are making their troubled way toward Earth is called a "Battlestar." It is a military command ship, the only remaining one of five built to defend the twelve planets colonized by the humans descended from the ancient Lords of Kobol. This Battlestar is named *Galactica*, a word that has a common root with words Earth humans use to refer to star systems or to gatherings of exceptional people. For those who observe the events on board the *Galactica*, the Battlestar is aptly named.

Not only is it a kind of man-made star system, but it is populated with men and women of exceptional abilities and insights. Most exceptional among them is their leader, Commander Adama, whose name is significant to Earth humans because it is derived from that of the legendary father of all humans on Earth. Adama symbolizes the "unredeemed man," as close to wisdom as a human can get, but plagued by an awareness of his own imperfection. He is a military leader, but he is also a man of conscience.

Commander Adama leads an extraordinary band of space pilots known as Colonial Warriors. The two most exceptional of these Warriors are the Commander's son, Captain Apollo, and a lieutenant known as Starbuck. To Earth humans, the names of these two men evoke images from their own mythology.

On Earth, Apollo was one of the ancient gods. He represented the finer qualities of humans—justice and freedom, healing and music and enlightenment. He was noted for both his physical and spiritual beauty, yet he was always unlucky in love.

In Earth mythology, Starbuck represents not a god but a man; one who has many minor failings and weaknesses but is forgiven all because of his native charm. Luck smiles upon him, and so does love, but he is eternally restless.

Most notable among the women aboard the *Galactica*, are Adama's daughter, Athena, and one of the refugees, a "socialator" named Cassiopea. Both are beautiful, yet each is quite different from the other. In Earth mythology, Athena is the name of the ancient Greek goddess of war, handicraft, and wisdom, the constant friend of the beleaguered traveler; paradoxically she is both virgin and mother. Cassiopea, in Earth mythology, was a human, a beautiful woman of such excessive pride that she was cast out into the heavens to spend eternity in supplication, her arms forever reaching out humbly.

Despite what Earth viewers see occurring aboard the Battlestar *Galactica*, the Colonials are not by nature a warlike people. They desperately want peace, but it seems to elude them because they also love freedom, and refuse to give it up to the creatures known as Cylons.

Long ago, lizardlike beings known as Cylons, now nearly extinct, created a race of mechanized creatures to carry on their war against the humans, known as Colonials. These

Apollo and Starbuck in a relaxed moment.

A Cylon™* at the controls of a Cylon™* fighter, in pursuit of a Colonial Viper™*.

*A trademark of and licensed by Universal City Studios, Inc.

mechanical creatures and their creators are determined to destroy the humans completely, and for a very petty reason—simple jealousy of the human life-form. The mechanical Cylons "see" only by means of a red-light scanner, and their speech is an echoing, emotionless, electronic rote.

After the equivalent of one thousand Earth years, the Cylons have come close to their goal. Taking advantage of the Colonials' desperate desire for peace, the Cylons have agreed to a conference, with the professed object of signing a treaty. As the Colonials' leaders—President Adar, the Colonial Commanders, and the Council of the Twelve—wait expectantly on board the Battlestars to sign the treaty, the Cylons attack, destroying all twelve colonies and apparently four of the five Battlestars. However, in later episodes it appears that one other

Battlestar escaped destruction—the Battlestar *Pegasus*.

Two of the valiant Battlestars destroyed in intergalactic battle, the *Atlantia* and the *Pacifica*, bore names similar to those of oceans on the Earth; and one other, the *Solaria*, had a name derived from that given the star the Earth revolves around—further testament to the common origin of the humans on Earth and those in space.

The twelve human Colonies in space bore names that are easily recognizable on Earth as well. Caprica, Gemoni, Canceria, Piscon, Sagitara, Leo, Libra, Aquaria, Virgon, Aeriana, Taura, Scorpio—all are similar to the names that Earth humans have given to the constellations visible in their night sky, the only twelve that the star appears to pass through during the span of a year.

These twelve planets were originally colonized by four distinct races of humans, precisely the same four that colonized their sister colony Earth. However, while racial prejudice developed on Earth, very little of the prejudice on the Twelve Colonies was based upon color. Prejudice did exist among these humans, but the most severe form was based upon social and economic position.

All that now remains is the Battlestar *Galactica*, and a rag-tag string of refugees who have escaped the colonies in anything that will fly—airbuses, rocket-powered taxis, interplanetary tramp steamers, and commuter space shuttles.

Witnessing this holocaust from Earth, the humans of the "lost colony" feel a great sympathy. From their own experience, they are capable of understanding how and why these events have occurred. They know no creatures like the Cylons, but they feel the threat of mechanical forces of their own creation—machines built to serve them that have insidiously begun to dehumanize their creators, threatening to destroy the most precious qualities of human individuality.

And in their own history, the Earth humans have known a madman very much like the Cylon Imperious Leader. Like the Imperious

Leader, a man named Adolf Hitler, in the fourth and fifth decades of the Twentieth Earth Century, sought to subjugate others and to destroy any who were different from his own kind. During that same era, Earth humans witnessed among their own leaders men like President Adar who, in their own goodness, were incapable of seeing the evil of others, being so willing and eager for peace that they would trust all the way to destruction. Treacherous surprise attacks, such as that carried out by the Cylons, have been common on the planet Earth, not just during the era known as World War II, but for centuries.

However, the Cylons are not the only evil forces faced by the space voyagers; there are insidious evils within their own ranks as well. Although they are a far more refined species than the Cylons, humans are still imperfect creatures. At his worst, the human can be as vicious and as treacherous as any other life form, seeking his own personal goals at the expense of others.

Most notable among the evil humans of space is the treacherous Baltar. Like that of the Earthman, Judas Iscariot, Balthar's greed and lust for power are so great that he is willing to sell out his own kind to achieve his personal goals. Without Baltar's ability to instill trust among the Council of the Twelve, the Cylons could not have managed the surprise attack that destroyed the Twelve Colonies.

Less evil in intent than Baltar, yet equally as dangerous, is the wealthy, hedonistic Sire Uri, who is so determined to have his security and his pleasures that he always chooses the easiest way out of any situation regardless of ultimate dangers. Sire Uri does not threaten his fellow Colonials by commission so much as by omission, by encouraging others to follow his philosophy of materialism, of ease, comfort, and blind acceptance.

Sire Uri's leadership leaves the space travelers open to the threat of the Ovions, who are working secretly with the Cylons. A communistic society, the antlike Ovions are under the dictatorial rule of Queen Lotay, and they lure the Colonials to their planet—Carillon—

by taking advantage of their materialistic, hedonistic nature. Attracted by all the gold cubits they can stuff into their pockets and by all the food and drink with which they can fill their bellies, the space humans do not see until it is almost too late that they are actually being fed upon.

The Ovions and the Cylons make strange bedfellows, since one is a communist society and the other fascist, but they have a common goal in seeking to trap the humans. The mechanized Cylons want to see the humans destroyed entirely, because they see their disorderly freedom as a threat, while the Ovions want to trap the humans to store them as food for their unborn larvae.

Even in this strange setting, the threats faced by the Colonials are familiar to those on Earth, suggesting that the human dilemma in space is

Starbuck, Apollo, and Boomer (back to camera) shoot their way out of a tight spot.

no different from that of those who watch the events, and that it is an eternal dilemma. However, it is encouraging to Earth viewers to see that their relatives in space ultimately triumph over the dangers and threats of their enemies, and to see that the qualities of human goodness survive and even thrive in the face of adversity.

Perhaps the most encouraging qualities the Earth viewers see in the Colonials are those of family loyalty and affection, qualities they feel themselves losing, and which they long to have returned to them. There are tender moments between Commander Adama and his son and daughter that the Earth humans find poignant and moving, because they are genuine, honest, and affectionate. That affection carries over to the relationships among Adama's children, best exemplified by a moment between Captain Apollo and his younger brother, Lieutenant Zac, in the midst of Zac's first mission in combat. Caught under Cylon fire, the experienced Apollo is impressed by his brother's valor under pressure, and he expresses his feelings openly, saying, "You can fly with me anytime, Little Brother," just before Zac is killed. It is the

kind of sentiment Earth humans often find themselves waiting too late to express.

Among the relationships aboard the Battlestar *Galactica* is one that is readily recognizable by those on Earth—that between Lieutenant Starbuck and Athena. Each has expressed words of love to the other before the cataclysm; in the midst of the doubt and uncertainty of their migration, they try to talk of their "future" together, but they find it impossible. Faced with the possibility of no future at all, Starbuck has difficulty in being constant in love.

That feeling is reinforced in him and in the viewers when Captain Apollo meets, falls in love with, and marries beautiful Serina, a newswoman who later becomes one of the first female Warriors. Their marriage is very brief, for Serina is killed in a Cylon ambush. She leaves behind a child from an earlier marriage,

Apollo and Adama land their Viper™* on Caprica after the Cylon™* attack.

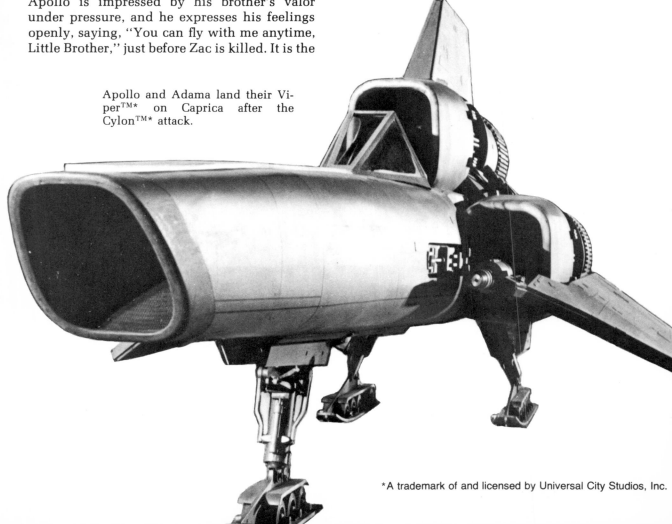

Queen Lotay, ruler of the insectoid Ovions, with one of her subjects.

a little boy named Boxey, who becomes Apollo's charge.

To the space travelers and to the Earth humans alike, Boxey represents the future of humankind. In his innocence and in his vibrant enthusiasm, he is hope; he is the victim of tragedy and circumstance yet he is determined to survive. Having already lost his father, Boxey is almost overwhelmed by the loss of his daggit during the destruction of Caprica. His daggit, of the same species Earth humans call a dog, was named Muffey, and Boxey loved Muffey as deeply as Earth boys love their dogs.

To help ease Boxey's loss, Apollo asks the Battlestar *Galactica's* doctor to fashion a daggit out of old Droid parts. At first Boxey is skeptical about accepting a mechanical sub-stitute. But the new Muffey seems capable of as deep a love as a genuine daggit, and the two—boy and mechanical daggit—become inseparable. However, when Serina dies, leaving Boxey an orphan, there is no way she can be replaced, and he and Muffey are adopted by the entire crew of the Battlestar *Galactica*.

The simple courage and valiant heroism among the passengers and crew of the Battlestar appeals strongly to those who view the events. On Earth, where for so long heroes have been looked upon with doubt and suspicion, the heroes of the Battlestar *Galactica*—Adama, Apollo, and Starbuck—reveal the genuine quality of men dealing constructively with adversity rather than seeking glory for themselves. Their gallantry exists not only in the

When Boxey and Muffey accompany Apollo and Serina to Carillon, they are captured by the antlike Ovions.

tension and fire of battle but in the subdued and gentle moments of personal relationships.

As the Council of the Twelve deliberates Sire Uri's proposal that the Colonials lay down their arms and settle into the easy life offered them on Carillon by the Ovions, the elderly Councilman Anton makes a significant comment on the idea of awarding the Gold Cluster to the Warriors who have saved their lives. "Just what we need at the moment, some old-fashioned down-to-goodness heroes," he says.

The implication is that heroes are not born, but created by politicians to serve nefarious ends. Most Earth humans would go along with that view, having seen so many empty heroes forced upon them, but there are those who consider heroes—true heroes—essential to maintaining the good and positive human values that can withstand the forces that would deny freedom.

Muffey, the mechanical daggit, is Boxey's beloved pet.

On Earth, the heroes of the Battlestar *Galactica* are rapidly becoming heroes of the people, freely chosen out of genuine admiration. The Earth humans sit before their viewing screens each week, observing yet another confrontation between the good people of the Battlestar *Galactica* and those evil forces who would abrogate the Colonials' freedom, indeed would destroy their very lives. They sit, and they observe, hoping to see good triumph over evil once more.

The preceding report on the state of the Galaxy was filed by an extremely gullible Earth human who genuinely believed that what he watched on his home television screen was indeed reality. It is important to point out that "Battlestar Galactica" is not reality, but the work of highly skilled artisans. It is not life, but art.

Boxey and Muffey are threatened with capture by an Ovion.

CREATING A GALAXY: THE ART OF BATTLESTAR GALACTICA™*

One of the objectives of theatrical and motion picture art is to create an illusion of reality. If the reality sought lies within the realm of fantasy or science fiction, the artistic challenge is a great one, for the illusion that is to be created must be both fanciful and believable. Such a creation demands the combined talents of a great many artists and craftsmen.

The artistry of "Battlestar Galactica" is a phenomenal achievement. From concept to writing, from design to construction, from performance to editing, the various abilities of

Serina, Apollo, and Adama, on the dead planet Kobol, survey the ancient pyramids that served as burial chambers for their ancestors.

hundreds of individuals are utilized to create a unique civilization in unidentifiable, timeless space. The effect achieved is of a way of life sufficiently like our own to be credible, yet sufficiently different to tantalize the viewer's imagination with questions of how, when, and why such a civilization developed.

The viewers of "Battlestar Galactica" willingly suspend their disbelief and accept its fantastic world as reality. If for no other reason, this alone qualifies it as a work of art. It possesses, however, innumerable other qualifications in each of its separate parts, in the achievements of each of the individual artists, some of whom are visible on screen, and some never seen by the viewers.

Glen A. Larson/*Writer–Executive Producer*

Generally a work of dramatic or film art has its origin in the mind or imagination of a writer. "Battlestar Galactica" began inside the head of writer and executive producer Glen A. Larson. "I let my imagination run loose, then prayed that the artists, technicians, and designers could get it all on the screen," he explains. He adds, "They did—beyond my wildest expectations."

Larson's concept went a step beyond the usual questions of whether life exists in space and if so, whether it might resemble human life. Assuming that life does exist in other galaxies, and assuming that it is like our own, Larson implies that the space life is actually related to our life on Earth. The viewer is left free to ask further questions about exactly how the two parallel societies of humans are related.

"In terms of the architecture of the ancient world, the Pyramids shouldn't exist," Larson suggests. "But they do. So the question is: Who built them? Who designed the fantastic highways of the island of Bimini leading into the sea? Why is it that so many different cultures share the same legends, like the lost city of Atlantis? Our story only hints at one possible answer.

"The exodus in space could be happening

Apollo, Baltar, and Adama, try to escape from the tomb, which is under attack by the Cylons™*, now under the leadership of the robot Lucifer.

now or a million years from now," says Larson. "Or perhaps these people reached Earth a long time ago and became our ancestors."

In any case such a civilization would have many things in common with the society created by Earth humans. A part of the common heritage of humankind would be a common base language. Of course, Larson could not have written in a language entirely created for the film; if he had, audiences could have understood nothing. But he did lace his script with words that are firmly based in existing languages, yet carry an unfamiliar ring to our ears. Such words as "centons" and "yahrens" for periods of time, "centares" for money, and "daggit" for a dog convey their meanings readily, while not actually having any meaning in twentieth-century English.

*A trademark of and licensed by Universal City Studios, Inc.

Larson also conceived space warships and the Battlestar *Galactica* itself, which he saw as "a city in space, ten times larger than the largest aircraft carrier known today, armed with weapons which haven't been invented yet, and may not be invented for thousands of years."

It was an enormous concept, one that would offer a big challenge to the special-effects artists who would have to fulfill Larson's dreams.

But perhaps Larson's most significant achievement with the script of "Battlestar Galactica" was his creation of characters, relationships, and conflicts that made life in

Commander Adama and the new Colonial Warriors—all women promoted from the rank of cadet.

Starbuck blasts his way into the Cylon™* stronghold.

The Ovions escort Apollo, Serina, and Jolly to their leader, Queen Lotay.

One of her subjects plays the harp for Queen Lotay.

space seem as real as life on Earth. Other films and television shows—from the silents to *Star Wars*—have striven for big impressive effects and have achieved them; but few films in the fantasy and science fiction category have achieved genuine human feeling and poignance. He has avoided the stock two-dimensional characters who speak cliché-ridden dialogue that is embarrassing to the audience as well as to the actors forced to speak the lines. In "Battlestar Galactica" Glen Larson has created original characters in original situations with honest dialogue.

"The most dazzling sets and props in the world aren't worth a damn if you don't tell an interesting story about entertaining characters," Larson explains. "The Battlestar *Galactica*'s corner of the universe may be a billion light years from our own. But it's an environment for every human characteristic—greed, lust, humor, self-sacrifice, fear, and maybe most of all, heroism."

The tremendous success of "Battlestar Galactica" is due as much to stirring human drama as it is to its special effects.

Glen Larson's list of credits in writing and producing for television is proof of his understanding of the human qualities of drama. The list of important and successful network series created, developed, or written by Larson is a long one, including such shows as "Alias Smith and Jones," "McCloud," "The Six Million Dollar Man," "Switch," "Quincy," "The Hardy Boys and Nancy Drew Mysteries," and "Sword of Justice."

Although Larson's auspicious career started in entertainment, it was in an entirely different field from television. During a school vacation, he joined a singing group known as The Four Preps, which became quite successful recording for Capitol Records. Three of the songs he wrote for the group won them Gold Records.

However, Larson saw his real writing talent as being in the field of motion pictures and television. One of the first scripts he sold became an episode of "Twelve O'Clock High." Soon after that, he sold a screenplay to "It Takes a Thief"; it was then that his talents were

Apollo, in front of the Battlestar *Galactica*'s™* electronic controls, draws his laser gun.

*A trademark of and licensed by Universal City Studios, Inc.

recognized by veteran screenwriter Gene Coon. This was the big career breakthrough for Larson and from this point onward he rose rapidly, from writer to story editor to series producer.

John Dykstra/*Special Effects*

The talents of many artists and designers were required to create all the special effects set forth in Glen Larson's "Battlestar Galactica" script; but, whenever anything was believed to be "impossible," it was known that there was one special-effects genius who could accomplish it. John Dykstra had already created the impossible for the motion picture *Star Wars*, winning an Oscar for his work. Before that, he had gained attention for the special effects he created for *The Andromeda Strain* and *Silent Running*.

Glen Larson had conceived the Battlestar *Galactica* as being about a mile long, large enough to house a space city. The Battlestar had to have podlike structures to house the landing bays and launching pads for the Viper fighter planes, and it had to have turrets from which the laser guns would fire. In addition, windows were needed in the command station from which could be viewed the panorama of the universe.

While the construction of the interior of the Battlestar *Galactica* would be left to the art department at Universal Studios, John Dykstra, with the help of his artists, Ralph McQuarry and Joe Johnson, had the task of creating the Battlestar itself. They pieced it together using the parts from numerous toy and model kits—from battleships, Sherman tanks, trucks, vans, and tractors.

Construction of the Battlestar *Galactica* cost $50,000 and required much painstaking and detailed work, but the result was a 72-inch scale model with thousands of electronic working parts. It looked real, and, on screen, it appeared to be as enormous as the spacecraft Larson had envisioned. Parts lit up, landing bays opened, laser-gun turrets appeared to lift, turn, and fire. Seen through the windows, hand-painted murals inside the ship gave the

The Android Sisters, a trio of humanoid female singers, provide entertainment at the Carillon Casino. Each has two mouths, so that when they sing the effect is that of a sextet.

impression of the human figures and complex machinery that operated the craft. "Designing them," explains Dykstra, "was like painting a picture on the head of a pin."

But the Battlestar *Galactica* was only one of many spacecraft that Dykstra and his associates had to create. The Cylon command ship, the Colonial Vipers, the Cylon Raider fighters,

Like fellow members of the Ovion group, this Ovion guard has four sturdy arms, which facilitate grasping his prey.

and the various refugee ships the Colonials used to escape the holocaust were also needed. An entire fleet of spacecraft, very few of them alike, had to be created—a total of 45 miniature spaceships for 300 separate special effects.

Creating the craft was only half the job. The vessels had to fly—or to appear to fly—in space, interacting with other craft, emitting laser rays from their guns and fiery jet-streams from behind. They even had to appear to explode when hit by the beams of another craft. And all the effects had to be blended with the film's live-action sequences, filmed with the life-sized versions of the spacecraft.

"There are several ways to turn that trick—from blue screen matting to sodium vapor photography. But to understand them takes an advanced knowledge of subjects like optics and quantum physics," explains Dykstra, revealing his background in science and engineering.

"Blue screen matting is a form of something we've all seen on television. A commentator will be seated in front of a blue wall. Suddenly, the wall will disappear and film footage of a news event will take its place."

To create the sequences of the various spacecraft interacting in the star-filled cosmos, a special computer-equipped camera known as a "Dykstraflex" was used. This highly maneuverable camera, invented by John Dykstra, can make a stationary object appear to soar, spin, loop, or dive. The computer memory-bank also enables the spacecraft to appear to shoot lasers and fire rockets.

John Dykstra's effects, however, were not limited to the vehicles of the film. A variety of living creatures also had to be devised. The lizardlike Imperious Leader of the Cylons had to have eyes that would beam lights, and a robot named Lucifer required a see-through skull that would light up to display the cogs and wheels of his mechanical brain at work.

Dykstra also had to create one of the stars of the show, the mechanical daggit, Muffey, the constant companion of Boxey. Dykstra had to create mechanical devices that would make him wag his tail, perk up his ears, and bark on cue, behaving as a mechanical dog.

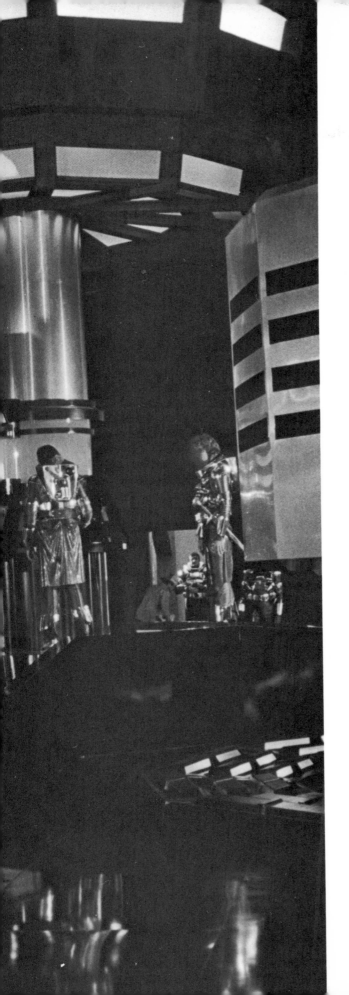

Art Direction and Set Design

The challenge was enormous also for the art directors and set designers at Universal Studios and their accomplishment was of considerable importance for "Battlestar Galactica." The average viewer of television and film is only vaguely aware of the contributions made by the many people whose names appear on the credits. In achieving the illusion of reality, the various artists and craftsmen within the art department are vital, especially on a production such as "Battlestar Galactica."

The illustrators, art directors, set designers, and set decorators are the ones who—with the craftsmen in the mill and the shop—create the physical surroundings in which the actors move. The illustrator is brought in at the very inception of a project to help the producers and the director to visualize the scenes that will be filmed. They paint scenes, complete with characters, or they build small scale models. The beautiful watercolor sketches by Bill Majors were very important in conveying the concept of "Battlestar Galactica," before actual construction work ever began.

All work within the art department is done under the supervision of an art director, and the sets themselves are planned and laid out by set designers.

John Chilberg was the art director for the three-hour pilot film. He worked with set designers John Warnke and Dave Klassen to produce the enormous functioning structures on the Universal sound stages, and with set decorators Mickey Michaels and Lowell Chambers to accomplish the final realistic details.

Perhaps the biggest single set that had to be built on the sound stages was the interior of the Battlestar *Galactica*. The most complex part of that interior was the spaceship's bridge, the command station, which consists of several levels and a vast system of electronic controls.

For those controls, Mickey Michaels contacted a large computer company and arranged for it to install three million dollars' worth of actual computers. Set designer John Warnke had to spend several weeks at the computer com-

The Cylons™* inside the generating plant for "the Ultimate Weapon"—a giant Pulsar cannon atop a mountain on the Ice Planet.

*A trademark of and licensed by Universal City Studios, Inc.

The shuttle crashes into the snow on the Ice Planet.

The Snowram is damaged when two of its convict passengers fight over possession of a laser pistol, causing it to go off.

A Colonial Warrior
with the Landram™*.

pany working with staff technicians to program the computers for the Galactica's functions, so that what the viewer sees is the real thing. In addition to the computers, other equipment was purchased. Included were flight simulators that are, according to Glen Larson, "one generation beyond the hardware in NASA's space shuttle."

A large number of television monitors, worth about $35,000 altogether, were also installed.

The sense of reality created by the functioning machinery on the Battlestar Galactica has a tremendous effect on the actors. Glen Larson explains: "When the Galactica is attacked by the batwinged Cylon warships and launches its own turbo-thrusters to strike back, the combat strategy is computer-controlled. Every knob, dial, and tele-light screen really works. The effect is dazzling."

That complex and expensive set was the cause of some fearful moments for the art department. Just before shooting began, Southern California was hit by heavy and continuing rainstorms, causing flooding on the ground floor of the art department building. Because of the numerous levels on the Battlestar Galactica bridge, that set was built on the "swimming pool" sound stage, which was even lower than the art building. There were fears that the millions of dollars' worth of computer equipment would go under, so sandbags were placed around the buildings, and water pumps were brought in and run twenty-four hours a day to get rid of the water that managed to seep in.

The Battlestar Galactica bridge was only one of numerous sets spread out across the Universal lot. There were the Council Chambers aboard the Atlantia, there were Commander Adama's quarters and his dining room. The Colonial Warriors Club Room had to be constructed, along with the Club Elite. There were the stark throne room of the Imperious Leader and the chambers of Queen Lotay; the glittering Casino, the Labyrinth, and the Incubation Chamber of the Ovions. There were Vipers, and shuttles, and Landrams. An entire strange new world had to be created.

With the continuing episodes of "Battlestar

The entrance to the Carillon Casino.

The Casino on Carillon, seen from above.

Decomposing human remains stored in hexagonal bins provide a source of future Ovion nourishment.

Galactica," that work continues, with new and different structures and vehicles being constructed each week. Richard James, who was the assistant art director for the three-hour movie, shares the responsibility as art director for the series with Mary Weaver Dodson; they alternate on scripts because of the enormous job that has to be done for each show.

They also have to adjust existing sets or use the vehicles in ways not thought of when they were originally constructed. The Viper became the center of a particularly knotty problem. It had to be placed on a sandbar at a location at the Fox Ranch, and the sandbar was out of the reach of any crane they could get. They decided that a helicopter would have to be used, and ordered one. The first helicopter brought in, a 47 J Ranger, couldn't lift the enormous Viper, and another had to be sent for. Meanwhile, with the cast and crew waiting, an entire day of shooting was lost.

Some of the problems the "Battlestar Galactica" art directors and set designers have to face are caused by the enormous scale of the spacecraft. John Dykstra had been working on the project for some time, creating his models, before the art department was called in to build the lifesized versions.

One of their biggest problems was with the shuttle. Taking Dykstra's model and determining a scale based on the size of its windows, they found that the actual lifesized shuttle would have to be at least 110 feet long, much too large to fit onto one of the sound stages. The art directors decided to construct only half the shuttle; but even that was too large, so they arbitrarily cut the scale in half, hoping that slight divergences in scale would not be noticeable to viewers, and built the exterior and interior 33 feet long.

The creators of the space structures and vehicles never seem to stop working on newer and more fantastic creations, surprising even themselves by coming up with more and more ideas. After the Landram and the snow sled, one might have thought that the creators would have run out of land vehicles for the space travelers. However, Dave Klassen, who was re-

One of the more unusual guests at the Casino passes through the crowd carrying a glass of Ambrosa.

sponsible for the shuttle, has gone on to design motorcyclelike vehicles called Land Probes. These were so complex that they could not be built from blueprints alone, forcing him to turn to clay to produce a sculptured version.

For a two-installment episode titled "The Gun on Ice Planet Zero," art director Richard James had to come up with the Ultimate Weapon itself, creating an enormous space-age generator sunk deep within a mountain, feeding the Pulsar cannon on top.

The giant generator consisted of five big metallic columns—one in the center, with four surrounding it—each containing an "energy pod." The energy pods were 17 feet high and 14 feet in diameter, and they had to move up and down the columns in concert like huge pistons.

"We were going to tie them all together and put them on an air winch," Richard James explains. "But somewhere along the line, someone decided just to rig the pods manually from above. That turned out to be quite a fiasco, because they found out that they had to have six or seven men to lift each pod, and to keep them moving in concert. When the producer's office got the call for that many special-effects men, they called me, saying, 'What the hell is going on? Why do you have to have thirty special-effects men for the laser station?'"

Looking back now, Richard James laughs. "But it was not a funny situation when it happened. Those things always reflect back on the art director, whether it was his fault or not."

Amazingly, with so many different people working full time on creating the physical settings, "Battlestar Galactica" has a consistency of style that makes it believable. It is a real world that is futuristic, but with traces of the ancient civilizations on Earth—a style which gives the show a sense of timelessness.

Jean Pierre Dorleac/*Costumes*

The subtle fusing of the modern with traces of the art and design from ancient Greece and Egypt is most evident in the costume designs by Jean Pierre Dorleac. Taking Glen Larson's suggestion that the interstellar refugees might actually have arrived on Earth millennia ago, Dorleac sought patterns of dress in the ancient world that might possibly have evolved from the needs of travelers in space.

The headdress of the ancient Egyptians was transformed perfectly to become the flight helmets of the Colonial Warriors. The ancient Greek chlamys became their capes. The Warriors' tucked and tufted shirts and jackets resemble garments worn by both the Greeks and the Sumerians. Despite the horrifyingly futuristic images of the Cylon Centurions, their armor seems to be based on the armor of the ancient world.

The amazing result is that all these details from antiquity seem to fit perfectly into the space culture; nothing is used simply for decoration; all the ancient touches seem to have

Boxey runs to safety from a predatory Cylon™* as Apollo calls out encouragement.

their place and function.

Jean Pierre Dorleac fulfilled Glen Larson's original concept perfectly, right down to the chromium covering for the Cylon armor. At one point, his sense of perfection almost became a problem. "Dorleac did the job so brilliantly,"

A Cylon™* patrols the Ovion chambers with drawn gun, stalking Colonials.

*A trademark of and licensed by Universal City Studios, Inc.

Larson recalls, "it became a nightmare for the cinematographer, Ben Colman. The chrome reflected every light on the set; it was practically blinding. But the effect was too scary to give up."

The physical preparations for the filming of "Battlestar Galactica"—the sets, costumes, and special effects—were a perfect melding of past, present, and future into a unified artistic whole. But, as Larson himself has pointed out, none of this would have meant anything without the human drama. The critical point—the ingredient that could make or break the film—would be in bringing the human aspects of the script to life.

And that would depend upon the actors and the director.

The clones of Ser Five Nine discover the Colonials unconscious in the thin atmosphere of their Snowram and take them underground to revive them.

The bride and groom, Serina and Apollo.

Richard Colla/*Director*

The direction of "Battlestar Galactica" was a great challenge on two counts. First there was the three million dollars' worth of complex electronic sets and machinery to deal with in a way that evidenced familiarity. Second there was, against this background, the moving human drama that had to be brought to life. Faced with this double-barreled threat, a lesser director might have been tempted to slough one focus off in favor of the other.

But not Richard Colla. He readily saw what Glen Larson was trying to achieve with his script, and set out to create a believable set of relationships among the space humans, and between the space humans and their machines.

Colla's first feature-length motion picture was *Zig Zag* in 1970, a thriller with a highly complex plot. This too was a director's challenge in its own way, and Colla brought that assignment off with an excitement that has

been described as "dizzying."

Richard Colla came to motion pictures with a solid grounding in television, having directed episodes of series such as "Ironside," "The Virginian," and "The Name of the Game." Earlier, he had won awards for his religious short films made for Family Theater. In 1964, *The Soldiers* won the award for the best short subject at the 1964 Venice Film Festival; and the following year, another of his films took first prize in its class at the Monte Carlo Film Festival.

"Battlestar Galactica" is probably Colla's finest directorial achievement so far. In fantasy and science fiction, directors often are tempted to press actors for theatrical effect at the expense of genuine drama. But Colla's respect both for the script and for the fine actors he was working with is clearly evidenced by the sensitive scenes achieved throughout the series, by both experienced and inexperienced actors alike.

After Baltar defiles the crypt of the Ninth Lord of Kobol the door closes on Apollo, Baltar, Adama, and Serina.

Colonial Warrior cadets aboard one of the Colonial Vipers™*.

Boomer and Apollo at the flight control panel.

*A trademark of and licensed by Universal City Studios, Inc.

THE GOOD PEOPLE FROM THE BATTLESTAR

There is nothing that unites people so completely as sharing a common adversity. Whether it is the common enemy of war, the upheaval of nature, or the deprivation of circumstances, humans are able to forget petty differences in favor of the interests and ideals they share, and that bind them together. The bond shared by those aboard the Battlestar *Galactica* is a common desire to keep and maintain their freedom.

It is that bond that also ties them to the humans of Earth.

The threat from the mechanical Cylons is a

As the wedding is solemnized by Commander Adama, Tigh gazes up toward the window, where a brilliant star is coming into view in the void.

continuing one, with the automated villains sometimes joining forces with other creatures of the universe. But always the Colonials elude them, keeping a fragile hold on their freedom.

It is a continuing saga, a form of art that traces its roots back to the *Odyssey* and *Illiad* of Homer in ancient Greece, and to the labors of Hercules in mythology. The characters of "Battlestar Galactica" are of the same heroic proportions as those characters in the ancient epics, yet they have an added quality of vulnerability that makes them seem real and identifiable to those who are alive today.

They have names that speak of mythical associations—names such as Adama, Apollo, Starbuck, Athena, and Cassiopea—yet they

Thane, one of the convicts, is captured by the Cylons™*.

Apollo and Starbuck talk over the plan to get to and destroy the Pulsar cannon.

have a flesh-and-blood reality that makes them familiar and real. Conceived in the mind of the writer, this reality is dependent upon the art and craft of actors for full realization.

Audiences often have to be reminded that the words spoken by actors are not actually their own words; however, it is also important to remember that those lines of the writer's could not live without the actor, and an inadequate actor is as bad as no actor at all. Even the finest actors cannot achieve the ring of reality without having a rapport among themselves.

While Glen Larson is to be greatly commended for his excellent script and for his abilities as a producer, it is the actors who must be given the ultimate praise for the vivid life of "Battlestar Galactica."

Above right: Boomer and Leda help Haals into the Snowram after he is injured fighting fellow convict Wolfe for possession of the stolen gun.

Lieutenant Jolly mans a laser gun on the Landram™*.

*A trademark of and licensed by Universal City Studios, Inc.

Richard Hatch/*Captain Apollo*

A young eager-faced boy in uniform pleads with a more experienced pilot to let him take the older man's place on a flight. The older pilot can claim anything—illness, fatigue, hangover—the boy doesn't care as long as he is allowed to fly his first mission. The lieutenant is hesitating on the verge of agreeing when their conversation is interrupted by the captain, who is—as it happens—the young boy's older brother.

The captain's name is Apollo, and he is aptly named. His green eyes carry a sensitivity and a wisdom unusual for one so young. His firm jaw and erect carriage bespeak vigor, strength, and action. And his wholesome, dimpled smile exudes love and affection. His appearance is as close as any human's can be to that of the Greek god Apollo.

Apollo knows what his younger brother is up to. He allows him to fly the mission, even though the young man is too inexperienced for such a responsibility. Apollo understands how his brother feels. He genuinely loves his brother, and he is not ashamed to express that love.

Love and understanding, valor and responsibility are perhaps the keynotes to the character of Captain Apollo. He maintains the balance between the "lyre" and the "bow," the balance between poetic soul and warrior of necessity that typified the god Apollo. He is an unusual character for the film and television of the 1970s because he represents a form of heroism that is not self-conscious or self-deprecating. He believes in life, and in the ties that bind him to other living thing; all his actions derive from the necessities of life.

It is a difficult role for an actor today to make credible, but Richard Hatch achieves the near-impossible, turning the god Apollo into a real and believable human being. In preparing for his role, Hatch researched the mythology of Apollo, and he believes that many of the qualities of the Greek god were written into Glen Larson's script. But, in discussing his role, Hatch offers a special insight. "Apollo has that one little quirk that is basic to humans," he

Apollo in his dress uniform, which he wears for his wedding.

explains, "a sort of craziness or nuttiness, a vulnerability that gives him a sense of warmth."

In "Battlestar Galactica," Apollo is the pivotal character around which all the other relationships revolve. He is both son and father, friend, brother, and husband. As the son of Commander Adama, he is the heir to a strong

Captain Apollo seems to be thinking, "Oh, felgercarb," as he hurries on a mission.

Captain Apollo checks one of the escape vehicles for leaks as the Colonials start out on their search for Earth.

The Colonials flee from the Carillon Casino.

sense of responsibility; and as stepfather of the child Boxey, he is the means of passing on that legacy.

Some of Captain Apollo's most tender moments occur with Boxey. The rapport between Richard Hatch and Noah Hathaway seems to be a genuine one, as close as that between father and son. Hatch readily admits that he enjoys working with Noah: "Some actors don't like working with kids or animals, because they always steal the scenes. But I really enjoy working with children. A child is less affected by the craziness of film work than an adult is. An adult actor goes through all sorts of mental trips from day to day. One day everything can be working just right, but the next day something may be amiss, and you're not quite sure what it is. You're constantly going up and down. Kids are not affected by that. No matter what's going on in my head, all Noah has to do is to look at me, and he brings me right there with him a hundred percent. He brings the best out of me."

As Hatch speaks, it is very clear that he

Apollo points out on the star chart the route he hopes to take.

Richard Hatch is highly articulate, and he takes his work seriously. He has only recently become a star on television, but he has been studying his craft and working at acting for thirteen years. His interest in the arts as a means of expression started even earlier, at the age of eight when he began studying classical piano, and continued for the next seven years.

He explains, "I gave that up because I was a jock at heart, and I couldn't stand to be in the house studying when I could be outside playing football."

There is some of the wistfulness indicative of Captain Apollo's delicate balance between artist and warrior.

Hatch grew up in Santa Monica, California, close to the surf, which always held an attraction for him. In his teens, while he was going to school, surfing, and lifeguarding, leading what many would consider an idyllic life, he was drawn to acting.

"To me, Hollywood was a million miles away," he recalls. "I thought of actors as mythical people that you saw up on the screen. They weren't human beings. It was only after I

means what he is saying. "I like working with kids," he repeats. "They're so giving and loving. They're not inhibited yet. They aren't short-circuiting themselves yet. Their emotions are flowing and free."

In the opening episodes of "Battlestar Galactica," Captain Apollo is married very briefly to Boxey's mother Serina, a newscaster from the planet Caprica. Apollo and Serina's brief, beautiful idyll of love ends tragically when Serina is killed by laser fire from the Cylons. The love experience does not exactly parallel the myth of Apollo, but it is in keeping with the spirit in that the original Apollo was always rather unlucky in love. Captain Apollo's affection is not spurned; rather, it is fate that intervenes. Richard Hatch explains, "I think that Captain Apollo is very idealistic in love. I think he's looking for someone who is very special, and he's not going to settle for anything less. In the case of Serina, it was fate that pulled them apart."

Captain Apollo, wearing his lighted Colonial Warrior helmet, gets ready for a reconnaissance flight in his Viper™*.

*A trademark of and licensed by Universal City Studios, Inc.

When Adama and Apollo discover how to get into the tomb of the last Lord of Kobol, they find Baltar has followed them.

started going with a few ladies who were into acting—I would go to plays with them, and to parties—that I began to fall in love with the atmosphere of the theater. But I still didn't see acting as a real, live possibility for me until I walked into an acting workshop in Hollywood that had been recommended to me. It was after I went to that workshop for the first time that I realized that acting was not just a mythical thing, that it was something that was very much human, an expressive art. It wasn't just make-believe; it was connected to real things."

Even then, young Hatch did not think of acting as his life's work. It was then simply a means of expressing himself, of getting in touch with his emotions. "Until then," he explains, "my only means of expression had been through music and athletics. I used to hold a lot of my emotions in because I thought it was un-manly to express them. In that class, I found that I could express my emotions, and that I could explore them. It was a way to discover new sides of myself and to grow, learning how to communicate ideas and thoughts and feelings."

Professional acting was still another world to Hatch, however, even after a year of studying. He was surprised when his teacher told him that he had talent and that he thought he could "make it in this business."

"I had never thought of acting as a business," Hatch recalls with a sense of genuine amazement. "I had just thought of it as something that fulfilled needs that I had."

The turning point for Richard Hatch was probably a visit to New York. Going to one Broadway show after another, he became truly excited about the theater. When he returned to Los Angeles, he was cast in a rock musical called *Allison,* which was aimed toward Broadway. Being cast alongside Ted Neeley and Kay Coleman (who later starred in *Jesus Christ Superstar* and *A Chorus Line,* respectively) excited him. However, the show never made it to New York.

Richard finally did make it back to New York with a group of actors and students who got together in Los Angeles, formed a caravan of

Apollo attempts to cheer Boxey, who is grieving over the death of his daggit Muffey during the Cylon™* attack on Caprica.

cars, and drove east. There were about thirty of them, and they formed a repertory company, renting a ballet studio on Eighth Avenue and 54th Street, where they would both live and work. After only a few months the company received an invitation to go to Rome.

"I had just gotten to New York," Richard comments, "and I wasn't about to leave. I was fascinated with New York. My agency was beginning to send me out for jobs, and I had classes in acting, movement, voice, and speech. So the rest of the group went off to Rome, and I stayed in New York."

The decision proved to be a good one. While living alone in a tiny room in the building that had housed their repertory company (with the bathroom four flights down), Richard managed to get his first professional acting job, one of the leads in a new soap opera.

"That was in 1969," he recalls, "and 'All My Children' was just being put together. Since I had not had any professional experience behind me, and this was going to be a lead role, they tested me about twenty times. I went through test after test, and they came to the one that would be the final, deciding test. I was so nervous I didn't know what to do. I was doing a scene with Karen Gorney, and she suggested we do an exercise before the audition. It was a reaction exercise: she would say something spontaneously, and then I would say something. It was wonderful that she did it, because it helped me to concentrate, and it helped me to connect with her. The scene went well, and I think the exercise that Karen had me do was the deciding factor. I got the job."

Richard went on from the soap opera to do an off-Broadway show, Love Me, Love My Children, which won an Obie Award in 1972. From that point, his acting career began to climb. Returning to Los Angeles, he began to guest star in episodes of television series like "Hawaii Five-O" and "The Rookies." Shuttling back and forth between the two coasts, he did The Last of the Belles, based on the F. Scott Fitzgerald short story; Addy and the King of Hearts, with Jason Robards, Jr., and a number of other episodes in shows like "Medical Center,"

"Cannon," "Kung-Fu," "Barnaby Jones," and "The Waltons."

He played in a movie of the week, The Hatfields and the McCoys, and in a two-hour episode for "Cannon," as Joan Fontaine's son; then Hatch was cast as Michael Douglas's replacement in "The Streets of San Francisco." After a year with the show, he returned to the stage, starring in P.S. Your Cat Is Dead in Chicago, where he was nominated for the coveted Joseph Jefferson Award. Then followed Deadman's Curve, the story of the rock and roll team Jan and Dean and finally, he was cast in the starring role in "Battlestar Galactica."

He likes the series immensely. "I've always enjoyed science fiction," he says. "For an actor, it's a terrific challenge. You have to imagine that you exist and function in an incredible imaginary world."

It appears that the series will be running for years, but Richard Hatch is not resting on his laurels. He continues his studies and looks forward to returning to the stage. "I enjoy doing film and television, but my most memorable experiences have been onstage. There's something magical that happens onstage. It can happen on film too, but it's rare. Even when it does happen, it can be cut for one reason or another. They may have too much film in the editing room, and they have to cut to get it down to the allotted time."

"There is a continuity onstage," he explains. "You go into the theater and do the whole thing straight through in two hours. Some nights it can be terrible; some nights it can be wonderful. If it doesn't happen one night, you can look forward to the next night. When it does happen, you can feel yourself connecting with the audience, you can feel the audience connecting with you and with what you're doing onstage. That's what is really exciting. With a film, you can't do that unless you slip quietly into the back of a movie theater and watch the audience. Even that isn't quite the same. You're not really sharing the experience unless you're up there on the stage, live."

With Richard Hatch's career now soaring, it appears that he will be able to enjoy the best of both worlds; doing stage, film, and television, all at the same time.

Dirk Benedict/
Lieutenant Starbuck

There is aboard the *Galactica* another kind of hero, a reluctant hero named Starbuck. While Apollo is serious and responsible, Starbuck is irresponsible and fun-loving—or at least he wants those around him to think he is. He is a charming rogue who lives for the moment and finds it difficult to keep his heart constant on any one woman, at any given time. Gambling, cigar-smoking, and courting beautiful women are his favored leisure-time activities.

As with other characters in "Battlestar Galactica," the name of this hero evokes images of other characters from other places. "Starbuck" is always an imperfect hero, more human than divine. He occurs most notably in *Moby Dick* and in the play *The Rainmaker*, and his name is indicative of one who "bucks" the "stars," who rushes in where others fear to tread simply out of necessity rather than out of gallantry or any desire for glory.

In describing the first mate of the *Pequod*,

Starbuck anxiously considers a problem, while Muffey looks over his shoulder.

Herman Melville says, "Starbuck was no crusader after perils; in him courage was not a sentiment; but a thing simply useful to him, and always at hand upon all mortally practical occasions." And in N. Richard Nash's *Rainmaker* Starbuck was a man who lived by his charm and his wits, daring the impossible, and depending upon luck to fulfill his dare.

The Starbuck of "Battlestar Galactica" embodies some of the qualities of these earlier heroes, and yet emerges entirely as an original, a kind of modern-day Everyman. Although the people of the *Galactica* exist in timeless space, Starbuck is a particularly timely hero for the Earth audience in the 1970s because the Colonials face many of the same pressures that present-day Earth humans do. Like many Earth humans, Starbuck finds that the only response to these pressures is to live for the moment. On Earth, he would be known as a "honcho" or a "good ol' boy," a man who laughs at the seriousness of his situation.

Dirk Benedict, the actor who portrays Starbuck, denies that he studied the earlier Starbucks for clues to his character. Instead, he has sought qualities in himself to apply to the role. He explains, "Starbuck is as close to me as any character I've ever portrayed. He has the enthusiasm of a young person, yet he's not unaware of the seriousness of a situation either."

"I really enjoy playing the character very much," he explains further. "Starbuck has a great sense of humor. He doesn't want to go into galactic battle because he loves the ladies."

Starbuck is rarely serious; and even when he is, he does not want anyone around him to know that he is serious because it might ruin his reputation. He feels a great deal of affection for his fellow Warriors, but he won't express it. In "The Gun on Ice Planet Zero" segment of the series, when young Cadet Cree is captured by the Cylons while flying under Starbuck's command, Starbuck goes to extreme lengths to get onto the planet where Cree is being held prisoner without anyone knowing his true reasons.

On one occasion, in the film that opened the series, Starbuck is hopelessly trapped, and it is a moment that reveals much about his charac-

While the Colonials flee the Casino, Starbuck holds off the attacking Cylons™*.

*A trademark of and licensed by Universal City Studios, Inc.

ter. Before the destruction of the Twelve Colonies, Starbuck had declared his love for Athena, Commander Adama's daughter. After the destruction, with the Battlestar *Galactica* fleeing through space, always one step ahead of the Cylons, everything changes, including the relationship between Starbuck and Athena. For one thing, Starbuck has discovered a "socialator" from Gemoni named Cassiopea; but perhaps more important is the impermanence and uncertainty of their situation.

When Starbuck walks in on Athena while she is changing clothes, she takes that opportunity to bring up the matter of their "future." Confronted with the question directly, Starbuck drops his humor and talks with her seriously. She tells him honestly that she cannot think about a permanent relationship in a time when the future itself is uncertain. It is a very moving moment, made more poignant by the fact that Starbuck is usually so glib and fun-loving.

A moment that is more typical of his character is his "discovery" of the Android Sisters. The promoter in him comes out. "When I meet the Android Sisters, a singing trio, each of whom has two mouths and two sets of vocal chords—resulting in some fantastic six-part harmony—I try to cut myself in for fifteen percent as their manager," he explains. "I'm the worst of the good guys."

Also typical is his desire to get out of work when he would rather be playing. When it comes to work, Starbuck has a knack for reading Captain Apollo's mind. In league with his fellow Colonial Warrior Boomer he frequently tries to sneak out of the room when he sees a particularly difficult or dangerous assignment coming. He is hardly ever successful at getting away.

As in the case of the mission to sweep the Cylon mines out of the path of the Battlestar *Galactica*, Starbuck accepts the assignment reluctantly, but once he is space-borne, he exhibits genuine valor. When he is out in space, with no one watching except others in the same situation, he can allow his true heroism to come to the fore.

"We are forever being chased," Benedict

Athena embraces Starbuck after his crash landing aboard the Battlestar *Galactica*™*.

*A trademark of and licensed by Universal City Studios, Inc.

Starbuck escapes Athena's wrath.

At moments such as this one, Starbuck and Athena are close, but as yet Starbuck cannot commit himself to one woman.

comments. "We go through space looking for salvation and safety. My character never gets the wind knocked out of him, no matter how bad things are. He lives for the moment."

Benedict never says it directly, but one gets the impression that his own approach to life is very much like that of Starbuck. He came to acting more by chance than by choice. He was hardly even aware of theater, film, and television when he was growing up in the Big Sky country of Montana. "I never thought about motion pictures," Benedict explains, "because we didn't have any. We didn't even have television. Every summer, they'd bring in a couple of old Audie Murphy pictures and show them at the Ranchers' Hall. That was our entertainment for the year."

Dirk Benedict's hometown is White Sulphur Springs, Montana, a small town with a population around nine hundred. "The entire population wouldn't have filled an average Los Angeles apartment house," he recalls.

He spent his childhood and adolescence hunting, fishing, skiing. "Throughout high school," he recalls, "I worked part-time as a logger in the Montana woods. The best thing about my growing-up years was that I learned to think for myself and do for myself. I had a wonderful father who passed away a few years ago, and he used to say that the educational process destroys people's ability to think for themselves."

Dirk's major interest in high school was sports, and he lettered in three of them before going on to play football at Whitman College in Walla Walla, Washington. It was there, during his freshman year, that he suddenly found himself thrust onstage, without really seeking to act. "It was on a dare," he recalls. "One of my friends on the football team challenged me to try out for a college production of *Showboat*. Since there was no chance I would ever be chosen, I figured 'Why not?'"

Much to his chagrin, he was cast in the starring role of the riverboat gambler Gaylord Ravenal. "I tried every way to get out of the show," he continues. "I pleaded with the faculty advisor, I pretended I was desperately ill,

I sang off-key. Nothing worked. So there I was on opening night, singing Jerome Kern's 'Make Believe,' and I loved it.''

As the result of that successful experience, Dirk decided to change his major to drama, and he continued to perform in the college musicals for the next three years. After college, Dirk went to Detroit for two years to study with John Fernald, who had formerly been head of the Royal Academy of Dramatic Art in London, and to work in Fernald's repertory company. "I never wanted to be a big star," Dirk insists, "just an actor."

After Detroit, he worked for two years as an actor in repertory companies in Seattle, and in Ann Arbor, Michigan, doing summer stock in the summers. But he didn't remain "just an actor." Not for long, anyway. He had, for a long time, been interested in music as well as theater. He played the piano and the trombone, and he sang. While he was in Seattle, he helped form a Dixieland jazz band. "I visited New York between gigs," he tells. "An agent there suggested that I attend a Broadway audition, just for the experience. I knew I had no chance whatsoever of being signed, but I got the part. I think the Dixieland band is still waiting for me in Seattle."

The part was in a Broadway play, *Abelard and Heloise*, starring Diana Rigg and Keith Michell, and it was a featured part. During the show's run on Broadway, Dirk was offered his first screen role, a part in *Georgia, Georgia*, a film written by Maya Angelou and starring Diana Sands. It was about draft resisters, and it was to be shot in Sweden. Two weeks after *Abelard and Heloise* closed, Dirk was on his way across the Atlantic.

After completing the picture, Dirk stayed on in Europe, spending four months in Sweden and three months in Greece, returning to the United States when his agent contacted him about replacing Keir Dullea as Gloria Swanson's son in the Broadway hit *Butterflies Are Free*.

This period was a major turning point in Dirk Benedict's career. It was also a turning point in his diet. "As a kid, I ate venison steak for

Starbuck (Dirk Benedict) a Colonial Warrior who enjoys gambling and the company of beautiful women, is one of the most courageous and daring of the Colonial Warriors.

breakfast, meat loaf for lunch, and a two-pound T-bone for dinner," he recalls. "But I found that meat was giving me the wrong kind of energy." During his stay in Sweden, he discovered a diet based entirely on whole grains and vegetables. While he was performing in *Butterflies Are Free*, Gloria Swanson reinforced his new dietary ideas, attributing her eternal youthfulness to her own vegetarian diet.

"I became good friends with Gloria and her husband, William Duffy," Dirk explains. "Because of her, I became interested in health foods as a way of life. I became a vegetarian and started eating a lot of rice, wheats, grains, and vegetables."

After doing *Butterflies Are Free* on Broadway, he was asked to do the play in Hawaii, with Barbara Rush. While he was there, he did his first television work, appearing as a guest lead in a segment of "Hawaii Five-O," which landed him another film role, the lead in *Sssss*, the story of a young man who is turned into a snake. He followed that with the part of Twiggy's wife-beating husband in *W*.

In 1974, Dirk Benedict was cast as one of the stars in a new television series, "Chopper One." Dirk recalls, "I starred in 'Chopper One' for awhile, but it got canceled. It was a very serious show produced by Spelling-Goldberg, so a lot of people had high hopes for it, but it was a show that drowned in technology. The starring characters never came to life."

After the show was canceled, Dirk decided to return to Montana to do some writing. He genuinely loves the mountains and the woods. "It's in my blood," he reveals. "I own a beautiful home on the lake there, on some acres. I grew up in an environment with cold winters and hot summers. When the spring hits Montana, you start to see green trees and you can smell it in the air. And there's so much hunting and fishing. That's what I miss when I'm in California. Part of me likes working on the ranch in Montana, and another part of me likes music and opera."

Now, with the success of "Battlestar Galactica," Dirk Benedict has exactly what he didn't set out to achieve—stardom.

Starbuck considers romance with Tenna (Britt Eklund), one of the clones.

Lorne Greene/
Commander Adama

When Commander Adama first appears on screen in "Battlestar Galactica," he is standing by a window gazing out toward the star-filled heavens, and he is troubled. The Council of the Twelve Colonies has just met to consider the peace offer from the Cylons, and Adama is worried by their idealism and wholehearted trust of their enemies. The Cylons were once living creatures, who have now become machines. Adama says of them, "They hate humans with every fiber of their existence. We love freedom; we love independence. To feel, to question, to rebel against oppression—it's an alien way of existing they will never accept."

He is talking about all humans, but when he says, "To feel, to question," he seems to be describing himself, for he is—above all others in the film—the thinking, feeling, questioning man.

As the commander of the Battlestar *Galactica*, Adama is a military man, but one of paradox. His entire life has been battle. The viewer gets the impression, however, that war is not a way of life Adama would choose, but one that has been thrust upon him.

The deeper part of his characterization stems from the image of the father. The name "Adama" approximates the name "Adam," the father of mankind on Earth. Like Adam, Commander Adama maintains the delicate balance of humans, a balance between godlike wisdom and personal doubt and uncertainty. The role is not an easy one for an actor to perform.

Lorne Greene portrays Commander Adama to perfection, giving one of the finest performances of his career.

Greene, of course, has had abundant experience as a father, both off screen and on screen, but that alone does not explain the sensitivity of his performance. Much of the credit must be given to his exceptional talent as an actor, for Commander Adama is unlike any father he has ever been called upon to play, since he bears on his shoulders the weighty responsibility for the

Commander Adama studies the ancient writings of his people, hoping to find guidance to the legendary thirteenth colony—Earth.

survival of the entire human race.

"This is the first science-fiction story I've ever done," Greene explains. "When I read the script, my first reaction was, 'wild.' Then I thought, 'But how in heaven's name are they going to bring it off?' "

Greene himself should be given much credit for helping to bring it off. Although Adama rarely confronts the villains directly, his character is essential to the credibility of the entire piece. All the other characters on the Battlestar *Galactica* revolve around him, depend upon him. Another actor, one more accustomed to science fiction, might have been inclined to overplay the part in an attempt to give the character stature and grandeur. The seasoned and sensitive instincts of Lorne Greene, led him to subtle and more effective choices.

There is a moment, early in the opening film of "Battlestar Galactica," when Adama has been pleading with President Adar to allow him to send out a squadron of Vipers to protect two pilots who have encountered Cylons. Adama does not tell Adar that the two pilots are

his own sons; and Adar, determined to believe the Cylons are sincere in their call for peace, refuses to believe Adama and refuses to allow him to protect those pilots. While the two leaders are talking over the intercom, Adar hears the loud explosion near the Battlestar *Galactica*, and asks, "What was that?"

When Adama answers, "That was my son, Mister President," Lorne Greene says it with an air of grim resignation that chills the audience, who knows that the young Lieutenant Zac is dead. It is the kind of line that, from a less accomplished actor, might have prompted laughs, but since the actor is Lorne Greene the audience participates in the terrible grief that Adama feels.

His determination in the face of grief is one of the important characteristics of Adama. The Cylon attack that begins with the death of Zac ends with the destruction of the Twelve Colonies including the planet Caprica, Adama's home. He returns there, to search for his wife in the rubble that was his house. There is an almost unbearable scene as he finds a group of family photos, and he says, "I'm sorry, Ila, I was never there when it mattered." For that brief moment, Adama seems overwhelmed; but suddenly duty calls, when a mob of terrified survivors approaches, attracted by the Viper. It is a crucial point in the story, the moment when Adama makes the decision to gather the survivors and to take them on a journey through space to try to find the lost thirteenth colony. It is a difficult scene for an actor to make convincing, making the transition from personal grief to public command. But Lorne Greene rises from the rubble of Adama's home with a mixture of gentle compassion and firm resolution, and the audience is able to believe him.

Commander Adama comes to life because of Greene's ability to perceive real human qualities in the midst of the fantastic, imaginary science-fiction world. However, much of Adama's time is spent in the command station of the Battlestar *Galactica*, on the bridge, working with the complex array of computers and machines.

"We have to deal with unfamiliar objects as if

Adama and representatives of the Colonies pledge their unity.

we've lived with them all our lives," he reveals. "Even in character, it's disconcerting to have a robot dog fix you with his laser-beam eyes, then cock his head to be petted. I have to imagine that this parallel world actually exists, that its social and cultural crises—and its fantastic creatures—are real. It's the only way to behave normally under abnormal circumstances."

Seeing Commander Adama move about the bridge coping with crises that come to him via machine, it is clear that Lorne Greene feels at home in the setting, because those moments are entirely credible.

But perhaps Adama's—and Lorne Greene's —finest moments are those with his two remaining children, Apollo and Athena. At these times, his fatherhood moves from the general to the specific, and he exudes love and understanding only slightly restrained by authority. These are moments that cannot help but recall the most famous father role that Greene performed.

Because of the television series "Bonanza," an entire generation grew up with Lorne Greene as familar to them as their own fathers. He played the role of the father on the Ponderosa for fourteen years, guiding his Cartwright sons and coping with their problems longer than most real fathers are able to remain close to their real sons. Lorne Greene's Pa Cartwright, however, did not remain static and unchanging over those years.

"I've often been asked how I could play the same role in 'Bonanza' week after week for fourteen years. But it wasn't really the same. As the stories developed, so did the characters. We tackled some very delicate subjects that would have been impossible in a contemporary setting—at least on television."

He continues, "When it was over, I played a few villainous roles—a devious, dissolute bishop in *The Bastard*, and a financial gangster in *The Money Changers*. But most of the scripts I'm offered, and accept, cast me as a decent guy."

At age sixty-three, Greene was contemplating slowing down his acting career to spend time with other interests when the role in "Battlestar

Commander Adama and Colonel Tigh consider the route they are taking. It may be a Cylon™* trap.

Inside the tomb of the Ninth Lord of Kobol, Serina, Apollo, and Adama decipher the inscription detailing the exodus of the thirteenth tribe.

Galactica" came along. Even when he accepted the role, he did not expect the enormous hit. "I thought I would work two days a week," he recalls. "But you can't say, 'Write me out of this,' or 'write me out of that.'"

He seems set for a second generation of television fatherhood, just as he has accepted fatherhood a second time in his personal life. (After rearing two children to adulthood, he is beginning a second family with his second wife.)

Lorne Greene's acting career began when he was quite young in his native Canada. He was in his teens when he decided he wanted to become an actor and began to cultivate his deeply resonant speaking voice.

"I was raised in the Ottawa Valley of Canada," he recalls, "where the people are a mixture of Scots, Irish, French, Indian, and several other backgrounds. The dialect there is so thick that it's almost another tongue. Words like 'about' become 'a-boot.' When I got the acting bug, at the age of sixteen, I knew I'd never amount to anything unless people understood what I said. I worked day after day for years to lose the accent of my childhood."

After studying at Queen's University, Greene went to New York where he received a fellowship to study with Sanford Meisner and Martha Graham at The Neighborhood Playhouse, the spawning ground for many of America's finest actors. Two years later he returned to Canada to accept a job as the chief announcer and chief newscaster for the Canadian Broadcasting Corporation.

Commander Adama addresses the people.

After serving in World War II he returned to Toronto and resumed his radio work, while co-founding the Jupiter Theater and founding the Academy of Radio Arts.

The 1950s were a particularly busy period for Greene. He had to divide his time among theater in New York, films in Hollywood, and theater in Canada. However, that very busy period began with television, when he performed the role of Big Brother in Studio One's production of *1984*. His first Broadway appearance was in *The Prescott Proposals* in 1953, and his first Hollywood film was *The Silver Chalice* in 1954, which was followed by *Tight Spot*. Some of the other Broadway appearances he made in the 1950s were in *Julius Caesar, The Merchant of Venice, Speaking of Murder,* and *Edwin Booth*.

Other film appearances before he accepted the role in "Bonanza" were in *Autumn Leaves, Peyton Place, The Gift of Love,* and *The Trap*.

In Canada, he performed with the Stratford, Ontario, Shakespeare Festival, and co-starred in a production of *Hamlet* for the Canadian Broadcasting Company. It was in that production that Greene first confronted the evil Count Baltar, though at the time they were on opposite sides of the fence, with Colicos playing Hamlet and Greene playing Claudius.

While he was in "Bonanza," Greene found little time for other film and stage appearances. However, in the years since, he has done numerous films and television specials, including *Earthquake* and *The Trial of Lee Harvey Oswald*.

He continues to look forward to slowing his pace and perhaps enjoying some leisure time in his Lake Tahoe home. It appears, however, that he may have to wait. The Battlestar *Galactica* might take some time to find the lost colony of Earth.

Terry Carter/*Colonel Tigh*

Second in command of the Battlestar *Galactica* is a dignified, efficient colonel, whose military bearing occasionally drops to reveal a sharp sense of humor. Colonel Tigh has a deep admiration for his commander but when Adama gives up his command for a brief period, the colonel takes over with a judgment and skill equal to that of his long-time friend. To Adama, he expresses reservations about his ability to run the ship as well, but it is clear from his manner that his concern is more for his commander, who seems to have sunk into a deep despair.

The moment when the two old friends discuss Adama's resignation is a poignant one. It is a moment when Adama's human compassion has overcome his military determination, and Tigh sees this, perhaps knowing that Adama will return when challenged. Tigh is willing to fill in for him and to step aside when the time comes.

That time arrives when the hedonistic Sire Uri foolishly leads the Colonials into the Cylon trap on the planet Carillon. Tigh is delighted to see Adama outraged by the situation. Since Sire Uri has assumed political control of the space refugees, he will be suspicious if Adama asks to rescind his resignation. Together, Tigh and Adama devise a plan.

Colonel Tigh accepts the weighty responsibility of commanding the Battlestar *Galactica*™* upon Adama's resignation.

Colonel Tigh, second in command on the Battlestar *Galactica*™*

*A trademark of and licensed by Universal City Studios, Inc.

Certain that the Cylons intend to attack while the Colonials are on Carillon enjoying themselves, the two plan to send passengers dressed as Colonial Warriors down to Carillon while keeping the real Warriors aboard the Battlestar *Galactica*, ready for defense. Tigh will go to Carillon with the fake troops, leaving Adama temporarily in command of the Battlestar.

Tigh is delighted by his friend's renewed courage and sets about implementing the plan by "borrowing" uniforms from the men without their knowledge. One of the more humorous moments in the show occurs when the superior, Tigh, is caught rifling the closets of his men. Thinking quickly, Tigh immediately rises to his full height of authority and berates the men for keeping their uniforms so sloppily.

Tigh makes a similar about-face during the festivities celebrating the imminent marriage of Apollo and Serina, revealing again the warm-hearted nature beneath his cold, efficient exterior. The Colonial Warriors have been caught stealing ale and Ambrosa from the officers' rations. The guard demands to know who is in charge, just as Colonel Tigh walks in. Quickly, he assumes responsibility and dismisses the guards.

Alone with the Warriors, he reproaches them sternly, "There's only one thing worse than lifting rations from the officers' mess. Do you know what that is, Flight Sergeant?"

When Greenbean replies, terrified, "No, sir," Tigh breaks into a wry grin and informs him, "It's getting caught lifting rations from the officers' mess."

There is great rapport between Tigh and the men, just as there is a rapport between Tigh and Adama. It may be that writer Glen Larson intended him to be the "tie" between the command and the men. Certainly, the Colonel is one of the few characters in the show whose name is not obviously related to mythology. That may have been done to allow the character to operate on several different levels.

There are two characters in mythology whose names are quite similar to Tigh's, and both may be applicable. One is Tiu, or Tyr, the Nordic god of war, brother of Thor, and the equivalent of the Greek god Zeus. He resided in the sky and remained consistently loyal to one side in battle, never wavering. The other character with a similar name was the Greek Tiphys, the helmsman of the *Argo* on which Jason set sail in search of the Golden Fleece.

Whatever Glen Larson intended, it is clear that Tigh is the perfect associate and friend to Commander Adama. It is also clear that actor Terry Carter is perfectly cast to perform alongside Lorne Greene.

Terry Carter's background and training are amazingly similar to Greene's. Early in their careers, both men worked as newsmen, Greene on radio in his native Canada, Carter on Boston's WBZ television, as the first black newsman in New England.

When he was growing up in Brooklyn, New York, Terry Carter had no aspirations to be an actor. As a child, he dreamed of being a doctor, but in college, at Northwestern University, he changed that dream to law. It was while he was

Colonel Tigh tries to convince Adama to reconsider his decision to resign as President of the Council of Twelve.

in law school at St. John's University in New York that he got the acting bug.

He had an opportunity to join the noted off-Broadway repertory company at the Greenwich Mews Theater in Greenwich Village, and he took the offer. He moved on to Broadway in 1954, when he accepted a leading role opposite Eartha Kitt in *Mrs. Patterson*, returning in 1961 in the title role of the musical *Kwamina*, which co-starred Sally Ann Howes.

He became familiar to television audiences during the three years he appeared as Phil Silvers's sidekick in the comedy series "Sergeant Bilko." It was in 1965, after the Bilko show, that Carter left acting to accept the challenge of newscasting in Boston.

However, the turning point for Terry Carter came a few years later when he found himself confronted with two opposing offers—one in news, the other in film. A major television network offered him a post as a special correspondent at the same time as a European film producer offered him a leading role in a motion picture to be filmed in London. He chose the acting role and moved to Europe.

After two years of living in Rome, appearing in European films and writing screenplays, he returned to Hollywood to accept a continuing role in the television series "McCloud." While he was doing the series, he also appeared in a number of Hollywood films, including *Foxy Brown*, *Benji*, and *Possess My Soul*.

He and his family now maintain homes both in Los Angeles and in Rome. Because of the tremendous success of "Battlestar Galactica," Terry Carter may well be spending much more of his time on native soil, and American audiences will have the opportunity to see much more of him.

Herbert Jefferson, Jr./ *Lieutenant Boomer*

Lieutenant Boomer is one of the three heroic Viper pilots who are awarded the Gold Cluster for clearing the Cylon mines out of the path of the Battlestar *Galactica*. He, Starbuck, and

Apollo are all good friends; and, in battle, become particularly close. However, Apollo's position as captain sets him above the other two in authority, so—when it comes to playtime—Starbuck and Boomer are best buddies, sometimes joined in their fun by Lieutenant Jolly.

Sometimes Boomer finds himself pushed to extremes by his pal Starbuck.

It is at one of those moments when Boomer first appears on screen in "Battlestar Galactica." Starbuck thinks he is introducing a pair of Gemons to a card game they have never played. Since Starbuck plays that game better than anyone else on board the Battlestar *Galactica*, he feels he is sure to win. However, Star-

Boomer fires his laser gun at a Cylon™*.

buck runs out of gold cubits and he turns to Boomer and his other friends to shell out for him. With an expression somewhere between incredulity and anger, Boomer asks to speak to Starbuck privately. It is typical of Boomer's luck that Starbuck gets his way, and an alert is called before he can win Boomer's money back.

Most often, Boomer and Starbuck are "volunteered" for special duties by Captain Apollo. Boomer has a certain amount of fatalism to his character; whenever he hears about a particularly difficult or risky or dirty job, he knows immediately he is going to be called. As soon as he and Starbuck hear of Apollo's plan to blow up the minefields, they know Apollo's choices for the job and the two of them try to slip away. Naturally Starbuck and Boomer do not escape. They both accept their fate, resigning themselves to its inevitability.

Starbuck is usually responsible for making it inevitable. For example, he is well aware that Apollo has been recruiting Warriors to inspect the Colonial fleet for solium leaks. When he and Boomer come across Apollo inspecting a vessel, he does not turn and go away, though this is what Boomer wisely suggests. Instead, he hangs around until Apollo volunteers them for the job.

Boomer's annoyance borders on disgust and he tells his friend, "Keep talking, old buddy, and you're going to get us in real trouble."

Sometimes his annoyance does reach indignation and disgust, as when he and Staruck discover the Ovion Casino while on a reconnaissance mission to Carillon. Starbuck wants to take some time to enjoy the food, the gambling, and the women. Aware of the starving people in the Colonial fleet, Boomer grows increasingly irritated. Finally, exasperated, he says, "Well, how do you feel now, sport? We have the run of the place while our people are starving to death."

Boomer has a serious, responsible side, which he does not attempt to conceal in the way Starbuck does. He also has a tendency to use his head a bit more often than his friend does. After they have been in the Casino awhile, it is Boomer who begins to figure out

* A trademark of and licensed by Universal City Studios, Inc.

Boomer and Starbuck are fascinated by one of the many varied creatures also relaxing on Carillon.

Starbuck and Boomer hop off the Landram™* to explore the strange terrain of Carillon.

that something is wrong with the set-up. Boomer is a realist; he figures there just has to be something fishy about a gambling den where the customers never lose, where all the food and drink are free.

Much of Boomer's time is spent in serving as straightman for Starbuck, but he does occasionally go out in charge of his own patrol missions. On one such mission to an asteroid, with Lieutenant Jolly, he contracts a mysterious disease, and lies in bed in quarantine, near death's door, for two episodes of the series. There is a tender moment, when Apollo and Starbuck visit him. Asked how he feels, Boomer tells them, "Awful, but it beats being dead."

He is still weak from the disease when he learns that the Battlestar *Galactica* and the forces that have landed on the planet Kobol are under attack from the Cylons. He struggles to his feet and reports for duty.

Herbert Jefferson, Jr., who portrays Boomer,

*A trademark of and licensed by Universal City Studios, Inc.

comes to "Battlestar Galactica" after a busy ten years of theater, television, and films. He gives a fine performance in the film, and sustains his characterization well in the series, making the two facets of the Colonial Warrior—fun-loving friend and strong, gallant fighter—entirely credible in one human being.

Herbert Jefferson, Jr., was educated at Rutgers University before going on to study drama at the Actors Studio and the American Academy of Dramatic Arts. His theater career started auspiciously in 1969, with appearances in the ancient Greek classic *Electra* and in a modern American classic, the Pulitzer prize–winning *The Great White Hope*, by Howard Sackler. The following year, he appeared at Joseph Papp's Public Theater in another drama destined to win the Pulitzer prize, the first off-Broadway play ever to be given that award—Charles Gondone's *No Place to Be Somebody*.

Later that year, he starred in *The Dream on Monkey Mountain*, at the Mark Taper Forum in Los Angeles. He went on to do the Phoenix Theater production of *Murderous Angels*, the play about the deaths of Patrice Lumumba and Dag Hammarskjöld, first done at the Mark Taper Forum and then taken to Broadway in the fall of 1971. Also at the Taper Forum, he appeared in Jean Genet's *The Blacks*.

Jefferson has appeared in a number of motion pictures, among them *Detroit 9000*, *Black Gunn*, and *The Slams*. He has become familiar to American television audiences through appearances in "Rich Man, Poor Man," "McCloud," "Columbo," "The Streets of San Francisco," and "Mission Impossible."

In 1976, Herbert Jefferson, Jr., again showed his talent for picking roles in plays that would later go on to win major awards, when he appeared in the world première production of David Rabe's *Streamers*, at New Haven's Long Wharf Theater.

It would appear that this knack for selecting successful scripts has now been transferred to television. Lieutenant Boomer definitely seems to be headed for a place in the hearts of American audiences, and Herbert Jefferson, Jr., most assuredly is on his way to stardom.

*A trademark of and licensed by Universal City Studios, Inc.

Maren Jensen/*Athena*

In ancient Greek mythology, the goddess Athena guided Odysseus on his long and difficult journey home after the Trojan War, serving as his constant friend and advisor, and interceding with Zeus on his behalf. She was as wise as she was beautiful, but she found it necessary to assume many guises to accomplish her goals.

The Athena aboard the Battlestar *Galactica* possesses many of the attributes of the goddess Athena, yet she remains essentially human and vulnerable. Her strength is the traditional woman's strength, which sustains the resolution of those about her. Unlike the others, she rarely has self-doubts. Only once does her firmness

A member of the ground crew holds Athena back as Starbuck makes a crash landing aboard the Battlestar *Galactica*™*.

Athena (Maren Jensen), the beautiful daughter of Commander Adama and sister of Apollo, is a female fighter pilot romantically interested in Starbuck.

falter: when Starbuck and Apollo are about to take the terrible risk of clearing the minefields, she tells her father, Commander Adama, "I'm sorry if I'm not handling myself well. I've never faced death before." Even then, it is not her own death she is concerned about, but the possible death of the man she loves, Starbuck.

Most of the time she, like the original Athena, provides the perfect example of strength and determination for the men she loves. One of the most endearing moments in the series occurs between Athena and her father. He has doubts about his decision to take the Battlestar *Galactica* through space in search of the planet Earth. Doubting his own ability to lead, he feels it is time to pass on the responsibility of command to a younger person. Athena chides him, telling him that he's "not the Warrior I'm used to. What happened to the joy of living to fight another day?" Trying to rebuild his confidence, Athena cradles her father in her arms as if he were a small child.

Another facet of her strength is seen when Starbuck's Viper is so badly damaged that he has lost control of it. The only way he can return to the Battlestar *Galactica* is through the use of the computers and instruments. Athena is at the instrument panel aboard the mother ship, and she is determined to run the check with him. Starbuck, something of a male chauvinist, is outraged; he wants her to turn the check over to Colonel Tigh. Refusing to take any nonsense from Starbuck at a time like this, she forces him to run the check with her, bringing him in safely.

Only after he is in does she allow herself any emotion, rushing to the landing bay to throw her arms about him, to ask if he is all right. However, her "womanly" lapse lasts only a few moments. When she learns that Starbuck is concerned only about finding her father to castigate him for pulling the Battlestar *Galactica* away from the Viper squadrons while they are in battle, Athena becomes enraged.

A fiery temper is another characteristic of both the human Athena aboard the Battlestar and the goddess of Greek mythology. When Athena's temper flares up, reason temporarily

disappears. Sometimes the result is serious; sometimes humorous, as when Athena discovers Starbuck in the launching tube, making love to Cassiopea. Enraged, she turns on the hot steam inside the tube, cramping Starbuck's style and also causing painful burns, for which she is, of course, sorry.

Her love for Starbuck appears to be Athena's greatest problem. It seems destined never to come to true fruition because of Starbuck's fickle nature. His heart cannot remain fixed on one woman, and Athena is the kind of woman who would require constancy. While she has only one serious rival for his affection, in Cassiopea, it is not just the "socialator" who has come between them—it is the war itself.

Marriage had seemed certain for Starbuck and Athena before the great war that destroyed the Twelve Colonies. Athena has noticed a change in her suitor since, and she is not one to leave questions hanging. When Starbuck walks into the locker room while she is changing her clothes, she takes the opportunity to ask him about their "future." He tells her that he cannot

Adama comforts his daughter, Athena, as she is overwhelmed with grief over the death of her brother Zac.

Athena and Adama contemplate the news that the shuttle has crashed on the Ice Planet.

seriously think about a future with any woman when it appears there may be no future at all. It is a very moving moment.

The next time she asks, there is more humor in the situation. Starbuck is in the gambling casino on Carillon; Cassiopea is with him, but she has left the table. Athena approaches him in hopes of patching up their relationship. Her efforts are almost succeeding when Cassiopea returns. Starbuck ends up losing both women . . . for the moment.

Because of its many facets, the role of Athena is a difficult one, and the decision to cast an unknown and inexperienced actress in the part was unusual and risky. However, Maren Jensen has proved to be an ideal choice. Not only does she have a classic beauty and an air of refinement and dignity, but she has contributed some fine and sensitive moments to her performance. No seasoned actress could have brought off the moment of truth when Starbuck and Athena discuss their future any better.

Maren was born in Glendale, California, into "a totally non-theatrical family." Her father is a physician and her mother works for the Los Angeles Zoo. "Mom's job," Maren explains, "is to generate enthusiasm for the Zoo's special programs."

Maren attended UCLA for three years, studying theater arts, and she did appear in several college drama productions, though she does not feel this qualifies her for stardom. "I did absolutely nothing professional," she says with humility, "not even the California equivalent of off-off-off-Broadway."

Not sure what she wanted to do with her life after three years of college, Maren decided to drop out, and took jobs waiting on tables and selling shoes. She didn't have to work at them for very long, however. Deciding to try modeling, she quickly found herself appearing on the covers of magazines like *Mademoiselle*, *Seventeen*, *Cosmopolitan*, and *Vogue*.

Her acting career began when a friend introduced her to agent Barbara Gale, who responded enthusiastically and began sending her out for television roles. Maren had done two commercials and one guest shot on "The

Cassiopea (Laurette Spang), "the socialator" who becomes a brave Colonial nurse.

Hardy Boys" before the role in "Battlestar Galactica" came up.

"I don't know why Glen Larson picked me," Maren reflects. "I guess he saw something in me that he liked."

It is obvious that he saw the same thing that the audiences see in her. In an age of look-alike beauties, Maren Jensen has a distinct quality that is all her own—a mixture of wholesomeness, intelligence, and feminine magnetism, a perfect combination for Athena.

She may have had to take a few extra pains in getting things right until she got used to working in front of the cameras, but her efforts were all worth it.

"It's been an incredible learning experience," Maren reveals. "No matter what you think you've learned in school, when you face a camera—a real camera—for the first time, it's different. There's no way to teach what I've absorbed simply playing scenes with people like Lorne Greene and Ray Milland."

"It sure beats waiting on tables," she adds.

It sure does, and this is only the beginning for Maren Jensen.

Laurette Spang/*Cassiopea*

"Cassiopeia" is the name of one of the constellations visible in the northern sky. It contains thirteen stars, and the ancients who named the constellations thought this one resembled a woman, seated in a chair, with her arms upraised in supplication. Legend has it that the original Cassiopeia, wife of King Cepheus of Ethiopia and mother of Andromeda, was too proud of her beauty, and was cast out into the heavens by Poseidon to beg for eternity. Her daughter, Andromeda, was later made a constellation by Athena.

The original Cassiopeia had three major characteristics—her beauty, opportunism, and pride. The Cassiopea aboard the Battlestar *Galactica* shares these characteristics to some degree, but she has other finer qualities that mitigate the lesser qualities. The only close parallel between the two is the first characteristic—beauty.

Cassiopea is one of the refugees who join the Colonial fleet after the destruction of the Twelve Colonies by the Cylons. She is from the planet Gemini, and she is by profession a "socialator." She explains that the profession is a very old and respected one on her planet, where men and women are permitted to marry only every seven years, and only under specific astrological conditions.

Nevertheless, some people do look down upon her position, and, once aboard the Battlestar *Galactica*, she finds the need to do something more useful and productive. She accepts a job as nurse to Dr. Paye. Like Cassiopeia in the heavens, she finds herself seeking to make up for her past, and she does so with a humility and an earnestness that make it easy for everyone to forgive her.

She first appears in "Battlestar Galactica" when Apollo, Starbuck, and Boomer are checking one of the refugee ships for solium leaks. The living conditions aboard the ship are miserable; the people are crowded together, sick and starving. The Colonial Warriors cannot understand the Gemonese language, and they ask for a translator. A beautiful blonde woman steps forward shyly to translate; it is Cassiopea. She is dirty, undernourished, and has a broken arm, which the Warriors insist upon having treated by the doctor despite the cries from the other Gemonese that she is a "dirty socialator" and should be "jettisoned with the dead."

When Starbuck learns that Cassiopea is a

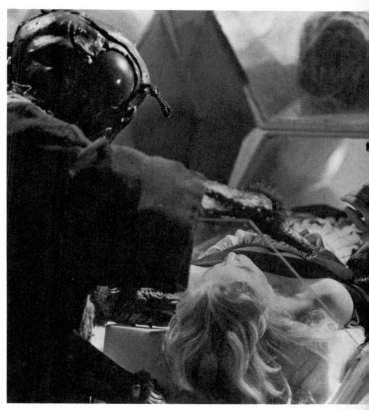

The evil Ovions prepare to place Cassiopea into one of the pods in which they store humans for future use as a source of food.

Starbuck is often drawn to Cassiopea, despite his considerable interest in Athena.

socialator, he takes a very special interest in her, constantly trying to find ways of getting close to her. He is responsible for getting her transferred to the Battlestar *Galactica*, where she can be more useful—though that is not his prime motive for doing so.

She is grateful to Starbuck for his help, and she is also charmed by his irresponsible, boyish honesty and good humor. She finds herself falling in love with him, creating a triangle that seems incapable of resolution, since Starbuck seems unable to choose between her and Athena. Each time Starbuck and Cassiopea attempt to be alone together, Athena somehow manages to come between them.

The first time, they try to find some privacy inside the launching tube, but Athena spots them on one of the monitors and turns on the steam. They next try to be alone while they are enjoying the hospitality of the Ovions on Carillon. Cassiopea leaves Starbuck at the gambling tables to see if she can find a room available. When she returns with the key, Athena has usurped her place alongside Starbuck, and he refuses to choose between them.

Cassiopea began as a secondary character, but has increased in importance as the series develops. In "The Lost Planet of the Gods" segments, she is firmly entrenched as Dr. Paye's nurse, looking after the dangerously sick Colonial Warriors efficiently and skillfully. And, after the death of Serina, she takes on a large part of the responsibility for looking after Boxey.

Cassiopea is played by Laurette Spang as a woman who knows herself very well, and refuses to adopt any pretensions or illusions—an ideal foil for the character of Starbuck. When she is coy or seductive, there are no doubts about her intentions, and when she is serious, she is deadly serious.

For Laurette, the role in "Battlestar Galactica" came as rather a miracle. It came after years of struggling to make it as an actress, without her career ever taking flight. "I hit the unemployment lines in 1976," she recalls, "and was evicted from my apartment. Finally I started getting some television work, and then 'Galactica' came along."

She first became interested in acting through a high school speech course she took to try to overcome her shyness, back in Ann Arbor, Michigan. At seventeen, she went to New York, determined to become an actress. With none of her former shyness, she managed to get onto the set of the soap opera "Dark Shadows," meeting members of the cast and asking for their advice and help.

They helped her to get a scholarship to study at the American Academy of Dramatic Arts. After completing her course of study there and practicing her craft in summer stock, she made the move to Los Angeles, making the rounds of auditions for television and films.

She managed to get a small part in the motion picture *Airport '75*, and made a number of guest appearances in television series including "Charlie's Angels," "The Streets of San Francisco," "The Six Million Dollar Man," "Happy Days," and "Lou Grant." She also managed to get work on special films for television, including *A Short Walk to Daylight*, *Sarah T: The Portrait of a Teen-Age Alcoholic*, and the pilot of "The Love Boat."

However, nothing offered her real recognition until "Battlestar Galactica." Even then, her part was not intended to be as important as it eventually became. It was only after the producers saw her on-screen in the rushes that they began to realize the impact she would have on audiences, and they began to change and develop her character.

Some problems arose because of her character's origins as a socialator, and some scenes had to be reshot. "The part of the socialator worried ABC," explains Laurette. "I had to be changed to Nurse Nancy." When they did that, she continues, "I got snickers from all the guys on the set. All of a sudden I'm dressed from head to toe. Before that, my outfits were slashed almost to my hips, I had four-inch heels, and things wrapped around my legs, very sexy. Suddenly I'm dressed to my chin."

The producers of "Battlestar Galactica" have high hopes for their discovery. Glen Larson reveals, "She and Dirk Benedict are going to be

Apollo and Serina ride a shuttle to the Carillon Casino.

The audience first sees Serina while hope still exists for peace between the Colonials and the Cylons. She is a newscaster, broadcasting live and in color from the planet Caprica, reporting on the progress of the peace talks, at the moment when the Cylon attack begins.

When full realization of what is happening hits her, Serina begins to call out for her son Boxey, who is running toward her, through the rubble, with his daggit Muffey. She grabs Boxey and holds him to protect him from the falling debris, but the daggit gets away and is killed.

Serina and Boxey are among the refugees taken aboard the Battlestar *Galactica* for the trek across space. Although she and Apollo have met before, on Caprica, their acquaintance deepens into love because of Boxey.

Unaware that Apollo is still carrying grief over the loss of his younger brother, Zac, Serina approaches him to ask his help in restoring

the Gable and Lombard of outer space.''

Jane Seymour/*Serina*

The Greek god Apollo had many mates, though none of his marriages or romances lasted very long. One of his most unusual mates was a human named Cyrene, daughter of King Hypseus, and keeper of his flocks. She was a beautiful woman, but she was also very strong, and it was her strength that attracted Apollo's attention when he came upon her wrestling with a lion.

He took her and made her queen of Libya, and placed her in charge of the myrtle tree, the ancient Greek symbol of death and of colonization.

While there are similarities between the ancient Greek Cyrene and the Serina of ''Battlestar Galactica,'' the parallel is not extremely close. Serina has an exceptional strength, but it is not a physical strength; rather she has a forceful and powerful way of coping with life and crises. It is perhaps this quality that attracts Captain Apollo to her.

Serina (Jane Seymour) is a newswoman and the widowed mother of a small boy, Boxey.

Boxey's will to live after losing his daggit. His help turns out to be just what the doctor ordered for all three—Serina, Apollo, and Boxey.

In the beginning, Apollo spends much of his time with Boxey, but, because he is near Serina, his affection for her deepens to love. While they are relaxing on Carillon, he proposes marriage, and Serina accepts.

They are not married in the opening film of "Battlestar Galactica;" however, they marry while the Battlestar is drifting through a great void, which Adama hopes will lead them to their mother planet of Kobol. It is during the wedding ceremony that the travelers first spot the bright light that will lead them to the dead planet from whence their ancestors came.

Some of Serina's best moments come in the two installments of "The Lost Planet of the Gods." One of the characteristics of the ancient Greek Cyrene comes out when Serina, along

with other women, responds to the call for volunteers to replace the Colonial Warriors stricken by a mysterious disease. Apollo goes to her quarters to see her; and, when Boxey tells him his mother is changing, Apollo thinks she is going to appear in her wedding dress. Instead, she walks out in the uniform of the Cadets, the Warrior trainees.

Apollo is incensed, but, mellowing somewhat, he tries to explain, "I love you. I don't want anything to happen to you. Ever."

Serina replies, reminding him of their positions, "Don't you think I love you? You go flying off into combat."

Serina
in her bridal gown.

Later on, however, she has a bit of fun with being a Warrior under her husband's command. When Apollo is being his most officious and commanding, she tells him, "I love you," embarrassing him in front of all the troops.

Another funny moment occurs after the women Warriors' first flight in combat. They are sitting about, recalling their various maneuvers the way the men had always done before, leaving Apollo and Starbuck out of the conversation. The two men facetiously talk about things that have traditionally been considered women's matters. It is Serina who finally asks if they are boring the men.

Serina and Apollo have a few moments of bliss exploring the surface of the planet Kobol together, but their happiness turns out to be short-lived. While they are with Adama in the tombs of Kobol, searching for the secret of the thirteenth tribe, the Cylons attack. Escaping from the tombs, Serina is shot by one of the Cylons.

She dies aboard the Battlestar *Galactica*, with Apollo by her side.

Actually, the main reason for Serina's death had nothing to do with the Cylons. The reason was that the actress playing the part—Jane Seymour—had to return to her native England for another role.

Serina and Apollo, newly married, pause for an intimate moment after landing on Kobol.

Jane Seymour is an extremely busy, and currently popular young English actress, best known for her highly successful performance as Secret Agent 007's one true love in the film *Live and Let Die.*

Jane Seymour was born in Bristol, England, and grew up in London, the daughter of a Harley Street surgeon. Originally, she had planned a career in dance, and had trained with the Kirov Ballet. It is lucky for motion picture audiences that she decided to change to acting.

A role in the motion picture version of *Oh, What a Lovely War* in 1969, was followed by *Young Winston* and a busy schedule of television appearances, including a continuing part in England's most popular dramatic series at the time, "The Onedin Line." She also ventured into film fantasy, accepting roles in *Dr. Frankenstein* and *Sinbad and the Eye of the Tiger.*

Feeling the need for more groundwork in the theater, she took a year away from the television and, motion picture cameras to do repertory, appearing in the works of Shakespeare, Shaw, Goldsmith, and other classic English writers. Without that experience, she doubts if she could have won the coveted role in *Live and Let Die.*

Jane Seymour feels she is just beginning to learn and to practice her craft, and is doing as many different kinds of roles as she can.

Noah Hathaway/*Boxey (and Muffey)*

The ancient Greeks always took along sprigs of box-myrtle whenever they traveled to colonize new and unexplored territory. Apollo made Cyrene, one of his mates, the protector and guardian of the sacred plant. Originally the plant had symbolized death, but colonists carried it to symbolize the end of one period and the beginning of a new. An evergreen, with waxy leaves, small berries, and tiny flowers, it came to symbolize rebirth.

It is highly unlikely that Glen Larson intended this small bit of symbolism in selecting the name for Serina's son in "Battlestar Galactica," but "Boxey" does seem to be an interesting and appropriate choice. He is an ever-present reminder of what it is the space-travelers are struggling for—the continuity, the future of the human race.

Boxey is—along with his constant companion, a mechanical daggit named Muffey—the most endearing element of the film and the television series. While death and destruction are all around, with the Cylons a continuous threat, the audience is perhaps most deeply and truly moved by something simple and identifiable—the grief of a small boy for a lost pet.

Boxey is a delightfully honest child. When Apollo tries to cheer him up by telling him that the Colonial Warriors have been looking for him to try to recruit him, Boxey sees through the white lie, saying, "I'm too little to be a pilot."

Later, when Apollo has Dr. Wilker devise a mechanical daggit to replace the original Muffey, Boxey looks at the creature—with mechanical ears, tail, and bark—with his eyes open. "That's not Muffey," he tells the adults straightforwardly. "It's not even a real daggit."

However wise he is, Boxey is still a child, with an open heart, and plenty of love still to give. He quickly warms up to Muffey, and soon they are inseparable.

It is clear, however, that the loss of the real Muffey is not forgotten. Like a real daggit, Muffey is constantly running off, invariably at the wrong moment, and Boxey is always running off to catch his pet, cautious because of the memory of what happened on Caprica.

When the Colonials are on Carillon, Muffey chooses a critical moment to run away, and Boxey is promptly off after him. They end up far below ground, in the Ovion chambers, just at the moment the battle breaks out. He and Muffey get caught in the crossfire between the Colonial Warriors and the Cylons. Again, when the Warriors are trying to load all the Colonials onto the Landrams to try to escape before Carillon explodes, Muffey runs away, and Apollo has to chase both boy and daggit to get them aboard.

The risks and dangers of the space travelers'

missions do not keep Boxey from living the curious and adventurous life of a young boy. When the Colonial Warriors, accompanied by a group of convicts, set out to the Ice Planet to try to destroy the Ultimate Weapon before the Battlestar *Galactica* comes within its range, Boxey and Muffey stow away on the shuttle. When, on the Ice Planet, the boy and the daggit are discovered, Boxey's explanation is "I've never seen snow."

Boxey is cognizant of the dangers, but he is determined not to let them interfere with the business of living. When necessary, he can act quickly and responsibly; he is alert and accustomed to the Cylon threats. Muffey quickly learns the traits of real daggits, and he too does what he can in moments of crisis. In one of the most delightful scenes in the show, one that prompts a cheer from the audience, Muffey at-

When Boxey is first introduced to the mechanical daggit, Muffey, he is cautious about giving his affection, but he quickly warms up.

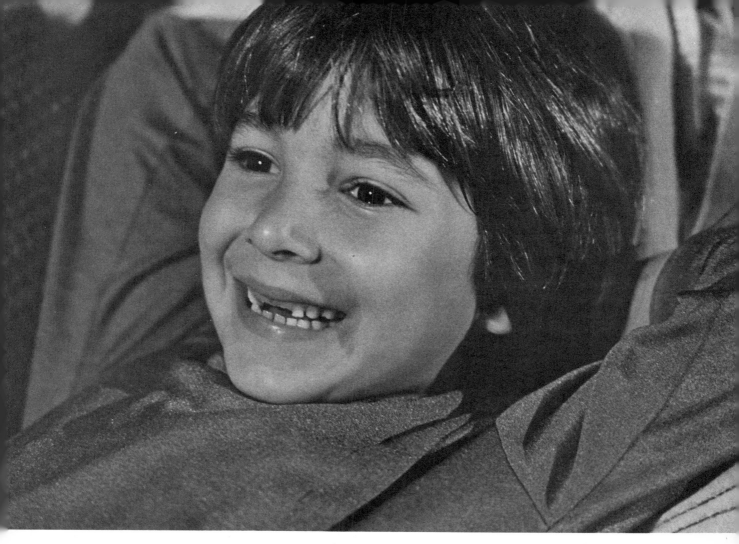

Boxey shows his happiness with a big smile.

tacks a Cylon, biting his leg, and short-circuiting him.

Boxey is also capable of some rather wry humor at times. When it appears that Apollo is never going to get around to proposing marriage to Serina, Boxey decides to get a few digs in. At dinner in Adama's quarters, with Athena, Starbuck, Apollo, and Serina present, he says pointedly, referring to Apollo, "I was told in instructional period that some people are just naturally slow." When his mother gives him a dirty look, he adds apologetically, "That doesn't mean they're actually stupid. They're just . . ." He pauses then and gives Apollo a meaningful look, adding emphatically, "slow."

Noah Hathaway, the young actor who portrays Boxey, gives a fine performance in "Battlestar Galactica," approaching his role with honesty, skill, and enthusiasm. At age six,

Noah is a seasoned veteran of television, and he has the ability—uncommon in child actors—to get deeply and believably into his role. It is also clear that there is a strong bond of affection between him and the other actors in the cast, and that warmth projects itself to the audience.

Noah is an adroit swimmer, diver, and acrobat. A student at the Lycée Française in Los Angeles, he also speaks French, making him perhaps the youngest actor in Hollywood capable of speaking English with an authentic French accent.

He has been seen in "CHiPs", the NBC special "I Love You," and on "America 2 Night," as well as in scores of television commercials.

It is safe to say that he is at the beginning of a very fine acting career, and American audiences can look forward to watching him grow and grow up on "Battlestar Galactica."

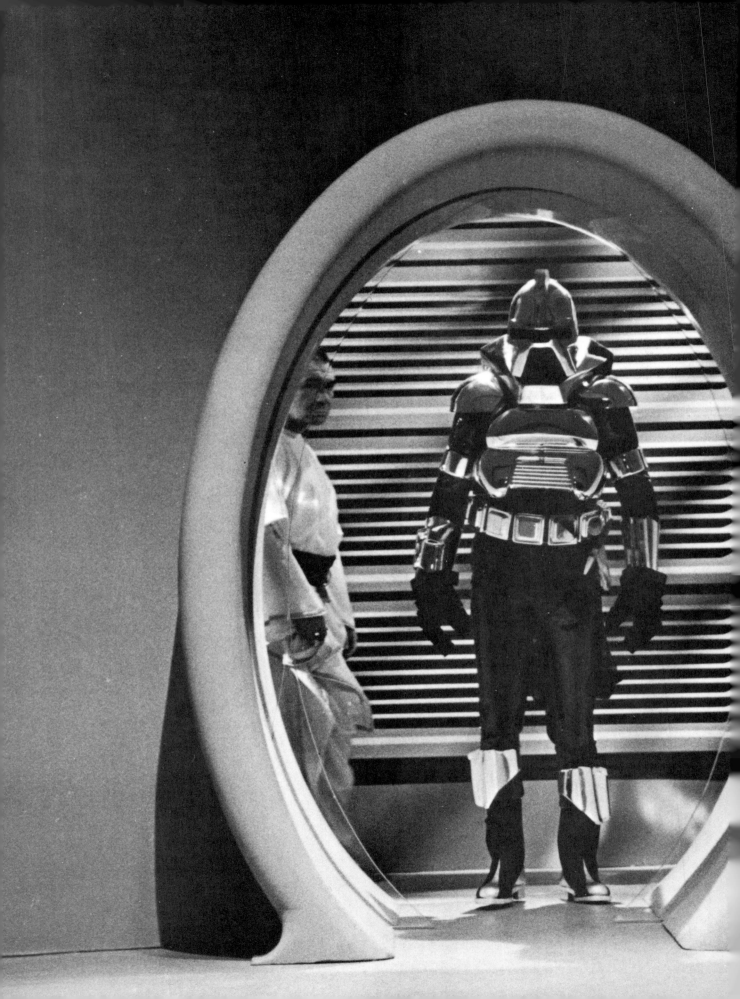

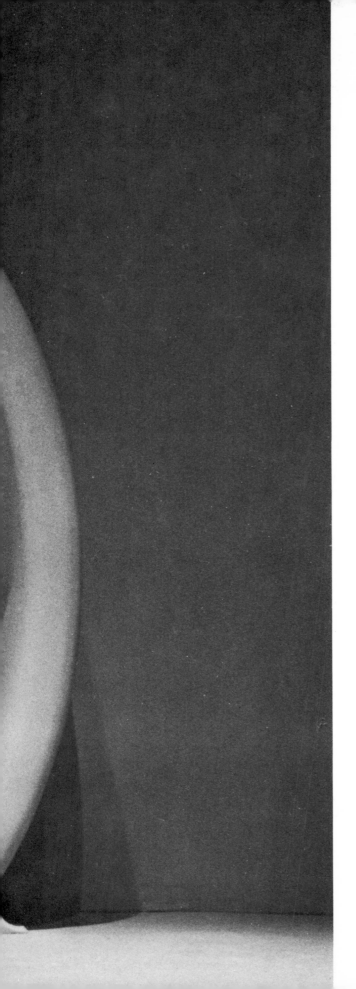

THE WEAK AND THE WICKED

In their struggle for survival, the Colonials face a multitude of dangers. Some of these dangers are clear and obvious; some are subtle, even unrecognizable to them, because they exist within their midst and grow out of the best of intentions. The space humans seek two things—the survival of the human race, and freedom. Their evil enemies, the Cylons, seek to deny them one or the other; the weak or selfish enemies within their own midst do not seek these same ends, but their effect is often the same. They simply fail to realize how they may be aiding the true enemies.

The Cylons™*, mechanical beings created by lizardlike creatures, carry out the commands of the Imperious Leader™*.

The Imperious Leader™*, the Cylon™* commander, sits above his Centurions on a huge pedestal.

The Imperious Leader™* and the Cylons™*

The greatest evil the Colonials have to face is the Cylons, who are living machines bent on destroying human life forms completely. The Cylons were once a rational and natural life form themselves, but their mechanical creations have taken over, and the original Cylons are almost completely extinct.

They began as lizardlike creatures, with exceptional minds but weak bodies unable to accommodate stress and physical hardship. Jealously they studied the human form to create humanlike mechanical replacements for themselves. However, there were some human aspects that could not be duplicated mechanically at all—the love of freedom, the appreciation of subtle differences among humans, the refusal to be subjugated as mechanically functioning slaves. Jealous of these qualities, the Cylons want to destroy the humans completely, now that they have mastered all the other human qualities.

The Cylons, however, have one quality that the humans lack, and it becomes a particular threat when they confront humans face to face. They possess a kind of sixth sense, an ability to tell when a human is lying or perhaps withholding some information when he speaks. Humans therefore have few choices when confronted directly by Cylons. Most often, direct confrontations mean instant battle with laser guns, and the humans have an equal chance. However, occasionally humans are captured without conflict for the purpose of gaining information. On these occasions, the humans have only two choices—to remain silent, or to find some way of telling the truth without telling the whole truth.

The Cylons are under the rule of the Imperious Leader, one of the last of the original species of lizardlike creatures. He is seen only when seated upon his throne atop a pylon in his darkened chambers aboard one of the Cylon Base Stars. Although the shining red lights of his eyes are visible, his head and body are kept shadowy, perhaps to keep the Centurions from perceiving how weak his life-form truly is.

The Cylon Centurions are always abject and obedient, approaching him with the obsequious salutation, "By your command," and repeating it as a valediction after he has given orders.

The role of the Imperious Leader is performed by a tall, muscular young actor named Dick Duroc, who began in "Battlestar Galactica" as one of the Cylon Centurions. His step up in the world began one day when Glen Larson visited Duroc's dressing room and announced, "Turn in your chrome uniform because you've been promoted. You're now the head lizard."

When asked how he went about portraying an outer-space reptile, Duroc replied, "You stand tall and slither."

Lucifer

It is incredible to believe that a villain could be lovable, but "Battlestar Galactica" does have one member of the evil forces who is beloved by audiences. His name is Lucifer, and while he is created by the Cylons, and is owned by them, he is not actually one of their breed. He is a mechanically created servant to the Imperious Leader, a superior brain intended only for calculating, without the clumsy chromium armor intended for warfare and destruction.

At one point, Lucifer informs Baltar proudly that he and the Imperious Leader were of the same IL series, a little in-joke that refers to Industrial Light, the original John Dykstra special effects company.

Lucifer's personality often seems more witty and humorous than truly malevolent. He has a superior brain, and he knows it. He seems to support the Cylon cause only because they own him, and he is a humble servant, created to serve. However, he does have a bad habit of occasionally "thinking out loud," of telling a leader subtly that he is being particularly stupid. Usually, it is the wicked Baltar who bears the brunt of Lucifer's truth. Because

A Cylon™* Centurion threatens the villainous Baltar.

Lucifer is never violent or even forceful. His smarmy voice is soft and smooth and even rather wry. He barely resembles a human form. His head is clear, translucent blue, resembling more a pointed light bulb than anything else. The viewer can see the working of his mechanical mind, and whenever a blue-lit mouth flashes on, it is always smiling statically. Only his eyes seem evil, when their red lights flash on.

John Colicos/ *Baltar*

The most despicable villain of "Battlestar Galactica" is not a Cylon or a machine, but a human. Baltar was originally a member of the Council of the Twelve Colonies, but he has chosen to betray his fellow Colonials in search of personal power and glory. A sort of space-borne Judas, he has sold the Colonials to the Cylons in order to spare himself and his planet. Baltar expects to be permitted to rule

Baltar is more evil than he is bright, he is usually too obtuse to understand what Lucifer says under his breath.

Because of Dante's *Inferno* and Milton's *Paradise Lost,* the name "Lucifer" has come to be applied as another name for Satan. But originally it referred to the morning star (or Venus), and its meaning is "light-bringer," referring to its appearance on the eastern horizon just before dawn.

It is hard to think of the Lucifer of "Battlestar Galactica" as being a representation of Satan. He is definitely the bearer of light or illuminating thoughts, but it is intriguing to consider the possibility that Glen Larson may have created him as the most subtly evil of all his villains, truly the representative of Satan as well as of enlightenment.

Lucifer's purity of thought, uncomplicated by emotions or feelings, totally subservient and without true loyalties, is enticing. He is the intellectual ideal, perhaps a suggestion that thought without feeling can be as destructive in its way as feeling without thought.

Below: The evil Baltar, seen in front of a sphinx-like sculpture in the tombs of Kobol.

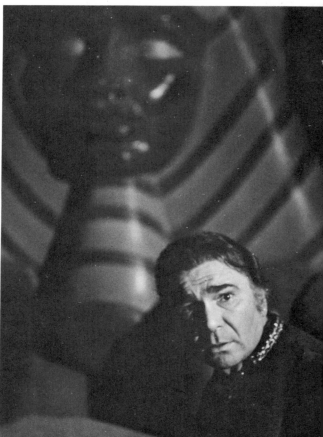

TOP: COLONEL TIGH WITH COMMANDER ADAMA.
LEFT: THE LANDRAM.™* RIGHT: A VIPER.™*

CLOCKWISE FROM TOP LEFT: LIEUTENANT STARBUCK; BOXEY WITH HIS
MOTHER, SERINA; ATHENA, ADAMA'S DAUGHTER; BOXEY WITH HIS MECHANI-
CAL DAGGIT, MUFFEY.

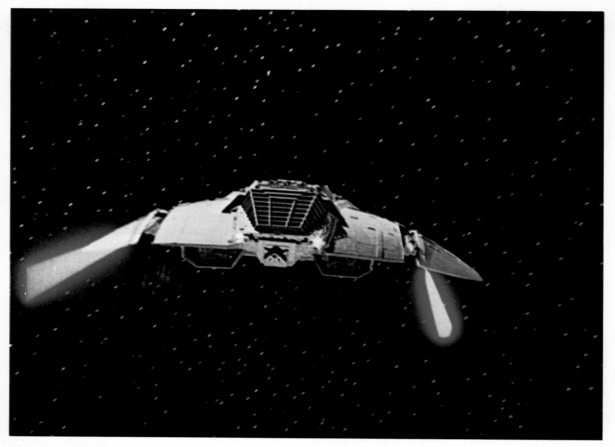

VIPERS™* AND CYLON™*
RAIDERS IN COMBAT.

QUEEN LOTAY WITH ONE OF HER OVION SUBJECTS.

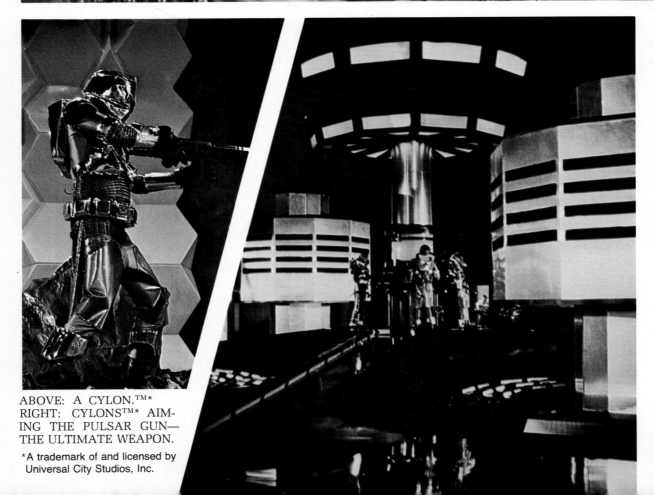

ABOVE: A CYLON.™*
RIGHT: CYLONS™* AIM-
ING THE PULSAR GUN—
THE ULTIMATE WEAPON.

*A trademark of and licensed by
Universal City Studios, Inc.

ABOVE LEFT: STARBUCK IN HIS VIPER.™* ABOVE RIGHT: CAPTAIN APOLLO. BELOW: A VIPER™* IN COMBAT.

*A trademark of and licensed by Universal City Studios, Inc.

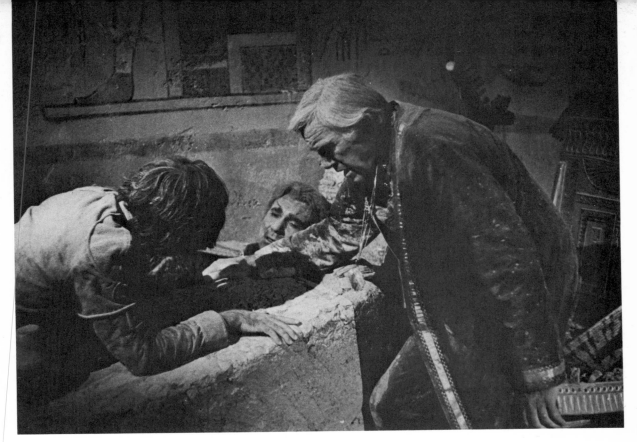

When the Cylons™* attack the tombs of the ancient
Lords of Kobol, Baltar is crushed beneath a stone.

the surviving Colonials as dictator. He does
not know that the Cylons intend eventually
to renege on their promise to him.

Baltar approaches President Adar and the
Council of the Twelve with the offer of peace
from the Cylons. Because Baltar is one of them,
the members of the Council trust the offer. They
are still trusting, even after the attack begins
and in spite of the fact that Baltar makes a hasty
exit in order to escape.

He is a wily and treacherous villain, capable
of any sort of duplicity, but he comes close to
meeting his match in the Cylons. Once the attack on the human colonies is complete, the
Imperious Leader is ready to have Baltar be-
headed, but there is one complication. The an-
nihilation is incomplete; the Battlestar *Galactica* survives. Using his wits quickly, Baltar is
able to take this piece of information and turn it
into his means of rescue. As long as the Colonials live, he feels the Cylons need him. He
knows how his fellow humans think.

When the Imperious Leader and his Base Star
are destroyed in the explosion of Carillon,
Baltar survives to serve the new Imperious

Leader. This new Imperious Leader chooses
to place Baltar in charge of a Base Star, giving
him Lucifer as an assistant. With Cylons under
his command, Baltar is given the charge of
destroying all his fellow humans.

Lucifer takes his orders from Baltar, but his
superior brain always finds holes in his mas-
ter's plans. With each attempt at destroying the
Colonials, Lucifer's predictions prove true, yet
Baltar never listens to his lieutenant.

When Adama sails the Battlestar *Galactica*
into the enormous void and comes within
range of the bright light that signals Kobol,
Baltar realizes where the Colonials are heading
and he hurries to the surface to join them. He
too is aware of the legends concerning the
mother planet, and he is waiting inside the
tomb of the Ninth Lord of Kobol when Adama's
party arrives.

Baltar is after the riches buried with their ancestors, but he tries to convince Adama that he
has been forced to side with the Cylons, and
that his true loyalties lie with his own race.
Adama wisely does not believe him.

However, Lucifer suspects Baltar will try to

*A trademark of and licensed by Universal City Studios, Inc.

change sides again, and he orders the Cylon attack while Baltar is with them. The tomb caves in, and Baltar is trapped beneath the stones, while the others manage to escape. The last words he speaks are, "You have not heard the last of Baltar."

And he does manage to return to his Base Star to command the Cylons another day. His next plan for destruction calls for the Battlestar *Galactica* to pass within range of the enormous Pulsar gun on the Ice Planet Zero. However, the Colonial Warriors discover the existence of the Cylons' "Ultimate Weapon" while on a reconnaissance flight, and the space travelers devise a plan for destroying it before the Battlestar *Galactica* gets within firing range. Once again Baltar is foiled.

The character Baltar does not exist in ancient mythology. Most likely his name is derived from that of the ancient Canaanite god of darkness and shadows, who came to be considered a false god when people began to worship the one true god, Yahweh. His equivalent exists under variations of the name in many ancient mythologies, perhaps suggesting that he was one of the earliest of divinities.

Baltar is played by one of the finest living classical actors, one who has—in recent years—come to specialize in villains. Like his old friend Lorne Greene, John Colicos was raised in Canada. Born in Toronto and reared in Montreal, Colicos began his theatrical career in 1946, and over the next few years played over one hundred roles in stock, repertory, and touring companies, including roles at the Montreal Repertory Theatre, Ottawa's Canadian Repertory Theatre, and the Brae Manor Theatre in Knowlton, Quebec.

In 1951, John Colicos went to London to join the Old Vic, ending his long association with the famous company in 1956 when he accepted Orson Welles's invitation to play Edmund in his production of *King Lear* at New York's City Center.

The following year, he joined the Stratford, Connecticut, Shakespeare Festival, appearing in *Othello, The Merchant of Venice, Much Ado About Nothing,* and *Mary Stuart.* In 1958, he appeared in *Hamlet, A Midsummer Night's Dream,* and *The Winter's Tale.* In 1959, he did *The Death of Cuchulain* and *On Baile's Strand;* and in 1960 he did *The Cherry Orchard* with Helen Hayes.

Colicos then returned to Canada, where he spent four seasons with the Shakespeare Festival in Stratford, Ontario, playing leading roles in *Love's Labours Lost, Coriolanus, The Taming of the Shrew, The Tempest,* and *Troilus and Cressida,* and performing the title roles of *Cyrano de Bergerac, Timon of Athens,* and *King Lear.*

In 1965, Colicos starred in the Broadway production of *The Devils,* and, in 1966, in the off-Broadway production of *Serjeant Musgrave's Dance.*

But one of his finest performances was in the role of Winston Churchill, which he created in *Soldiers* in 1968. He appeared in that play on Broadway, and in Toronto, Dublin, and London.

It was after that performance that Colicos turned his talents and efforts toward television and motion pictures. He has given memorable performances in such films as *Anne of a Thousand Days, Doctors' Wives, Raid on Rommel, Wrath of God, Scorpio,* and *Red Sky at Morning.* Some of his television appearances have been in "Petrocelli," "Harry O," "Hawaii Five-O," "Gunsmoke," "Medical Center," and "Bronk."

But perhaps his finest performance as a villain is the one he gives in "Battlestar Galactica." Colicos says of the character he plays, "Baltar is the most scurrilous character I've ever portrayed. For sheer awfulness on a scale of one to ten, he's a fifteen. He's the Benedict Arnold of the distant future, a kind of Galactic Judas. But he doesn't merely betray a few close friends; he sells out the entire human race."

It is an interesting reunion for John Colicos and Lorne Greene. Very early in their careers, their positions were reversed, when Colicos played Hamlet to Greene's wicked King Claudius. "That was before Lorne became a hero in 'Bonanza,' and I discovered that villains, like blondes, have more fun," Colicos recalls. "Inevitably we both wound up in Hollywood, where we renewed our friendship. But by then, the die was cast. Lorne was a Western father figure, and I was on the side of evil and injustice."

Colicos does give a magnificent performance as the terrible Baltar, and his role has grown with the episodes. Beginning with simple greed and lust for power, Baltar's evil has become so ingrained by the time he directs the Colonials to the Ice Planet Zero, madness seems to have taken over, and the figure that now sits upon the command pylon within the Base Star looks down with such an intense gaze of evil that he is positively chilling.

Ray Milland/*Sire Uri*

The villainy of Sire Uri is subtle, perhaps even unintentional—all he really wants is to be permitted to enjoy his sensual pleasures. He believes that the war with the Cylons is entirely the fault of the human military, and seems rather grateful for the destruction of the colonies, for it has rid him of his wife, Siress Uri. Now that that has been accomplished, he sees the military rule of Commander Adama and the new Council of the Twelve (of which he is a member) as a threat to his way of life.

In the refugee fleet, his ship, the *Rising Star*, has become the haven for all of those Sire Uri considers to be "the best people." He has formed a club, called the Club Elite, and he has posted guards at the doors to keep out the uninvited. He is hoarding food while other refugees are starving, and he keeps the merriment in the Club Elite going around the clock, with wine, women, and all kinds of entertainment.

Apollo hears of this from one of the starving refugees, and he and Boomer go to investigate, finding it necessary to force their way past the

Sire Uri (Ray Milland) is a Colonial politician who prefers pleasure to the harsh realities of the Colonials' endangered existence.

guard at the door. When Apollo has his troops confiscate the vast stores of food, Sire Uri threatens to ruin the captain. Sire Uri formulates his plan slowly, beginning by undermining the Council of the Twelve's confidence in Adama. When Adama announces his intention to resign his command, Uri enthusiastically urges the Council to accept the resignation, saying smugly, "I think our dear Adama is best qualified to judge his own capacity to lead."

Now that he has to suffer the privations that other passengers do, Uri wants to stop the ships at the nearest planet, Borallus, where he can replenish his food supplies. He does not approve of Adama's plan to go to Carillon where the fleet can also replenish its energy supply needed to continue on in search of Earth. Adama, however, is sure that a Cylon task force is waiting on Borallus.

It is Apollo who comes up with a compromise that is acceptable to Sire Uri. He presents a plan for the Battlestar *Galactica* to take a shorter route to Carillon through the Cylon minefields, which he and two other volunteers (Starbuck and Boomer) will clear.

Sire Uri is delighted with the discovery of the Carillon Casino. It is entirely to his hedonistic liking. Totally oblivious to the dangers of the planet, he is determined that the travels should stop here. With Adama "retired," he has the Council of the Twelve under his influence, and he devises a plan to get rid of the military entirely.

In a big celebration on Carillon, the three Viper pilots who cleared the minefields will be honored with the Gold Cluster. Sire Uri will use the emotions of the moment to convince the Colonials to lay down their arms forever, to convince them that the Cylons will not harm them if they are sure their intentions are peaceful.

"If we mind our own business, there is every reason to believe the Cylons will leave us alone," he says.

On Carillon, his plans are foiled by a Cylon attack, an attack that he does not believe is actually occurring until he himself is confronted by a Cylon Centurion firing his laser pistol.

The actor who plays the role of Sire Uri is one of Hollywood's finest and most respected, Ray Milland, who has appeared in nearly a hundred major motion pictures over a period of close to fifty years.

He was born Raymond Truscott-Jones in Neath, Wales, and insists on being referred to as a Welshman rather than as an Englishman. He was educated at Kings College, and the University of Wales, after which he served in the Household Cavalry. He began his acting career in England, using the name Spike Milland, in a movie entitled *The Plaything*. After several British films, he came to the attention of executives at MGM, and he was brought to Hollywood to co-star with Marion Davies in *The Bachelor Father* in 1931.

During his first year in Hollywood he made a total of five films. He quickly became known for playing suave, debonair, sophisticated roles. He had good looks, charm, vibrant eyes, and fine manners, all of the things that thrilled the female audiences in the 1930s. He also had a fine talent as an actor, but it took a while for him to get the roles that would truly challenge that talent.

William Wellman gave him two of his earliest chances to break away from the matinee idol mold, in *Men with Wings* (1938) and *Beau Geste* (1939). His performance made *Beau Geste* one of the great classics of all time.

However, his most shining performance is the one for which he won the Academy Award as Best Actor for the year 1945, portraying the alcoholic in *The Lost Weekend*. He brought to the role a subtlety and a sensitivity that made the character of Don Birnham come alive. Attention was first brought to the film by the very shocking nature of the subject matter, but it has remained as one of the great film classics because of the many facets of the alcoholic character that Ray Milland was able to reveal.

In the years since, Milland has played the widest range of roles possible, everything from comedy to science fiction to historical drama and suspense, giving many memorable performances, including those in *The Big Clock*, *Rhubarb*, *Dial M for Murder*, *The Ministry of*

President Adar and all the forces aboard the *Atlantia* are destroyed by the surprise Cylon™* attack.

Fear, The Man Alone, The Girl in the Red Velvet Swing, Panic in the Year Zero, and *Love Story.* During the 1950s, he also tried and proved his abilities as a director, doing *Lisbon* in 1956, and *The Safecracker* in 1958.

He is familiar to television viewers as the star of two highly successful series, "Markham" and "McNulty."

In "Battlestar Galactica," Ray Milland gives a delightful portrait of a self-centered, self-satisfied pleasure-seeker. His Sire Uri is a despicable character whose evil is neatly tucked away beneath his superficial charm. Because of Milland's great talent, he is able to turn a "guest-starring" cameo role into a truly memorable characterization, and Sire Uri is a villain the audience is not likely to forget.

Lew Ayres/*President Adar*

Very early in "Battlestar Galactica," the white-robed figure of a good and gentle man fills the screen, his face beaming love and beneficence. It is President Adar, who bears the

responsibility for governing the Twelve Colonies, and he appears to be all that is good in man. His power is tempered with gentleness; his strength is guided by wisdom. He seems to listen to every point of view before he makes a decision, and he seems to care about everyone he meets.

He is not in any way a villain, nor is he really weak, but his goodness is so deep-rooted and so pure that it finally destroys him and the civilization of the Twelve Colonies as well. Like Neville Chamberlain before World War II, President Adar wants peace so devoutly that he is willing to trust all the way to destruction.

It is an interesting character, and an interesting role for veteran actor Lew Ayres, who has always been a pacifist himself.

President Adar and Commander Adama are old and close friends. There seems to be a bond of love and trust between them, but Adar differs with his old friend on the matter of peace. He feels he must listen to Baltar in hopes of ending the thousand-year war with the Cylons. Even when Adama reports that the Cylons are attacking, Adar holds out, trying to rationalize it as something other than what it is. By the time he realizes his folly, it is too late. Within moments, his ship, the *Atlantia*, is destroyed.

Lew Ayres was born Lewis Ayer, in Minneapolis, Minnesota, and he did not intend to be an actor. He was studying medicine at the University of Arizona when a talent scout spotted him in a college production. That was in 1929, and before that year was out he was in Hollywood in movies. His first movie that year was *The Sophomore*, directed by Leo McCarey, and that was followed quickly by *The Kiss*, opposite the exciting new star Greta Garbo.

The following year, he created one of the most moving and memorable characters in screen history, the war-weary soldier in the Academy Award–winning *All Quiet on the Western Front*. He was one of the most sought-after young stars in the early 1930s, appearing in one hit film after another, including *State Fair* in 1933, *Shakedown* in 1936, and *Holiday* in 1938, co-starring with Cary Grant and Katharine Hepburn.

Councillor Anton (Wilfrid Hyde-White) is in favor of Apollo's plan to destroy the Cylon™* minefield so the Colonials can take the short route to Carillon.

But it was in that year, 1938, that he created a role that would be so successful that audiences would demand that he repeat it again and again. The film was *Young Doctor Kildare*, and Lew Ayres of course played the title role, with Lionel Barrymore as Dr. Gillespie and Laraine Day as his nurse. Between 1938 and 1941, Lew Ayres was called upon to do eight sequels to that first Dr. Kildare film. Only World War II could put an end to his performing the role.

When the United States entered the war, Lew Ayres found that he had to state publicly his religious conviction that would not permit him to kill. His studio, MGM, was upset that he was throwing away his career, but Ayres stuck by his convictions and volunteered for medical corps duty. (In hopes of salvaging the Kildare series, the studio quickly made *Calling Dr. Gillespie*, without Ayres, but it was not successful.) His last film for five years was *Fingers at the Window*, made in 1941.

The studio's fears that Ayres was destroying his career proved to be groundless. The Ameri-

*A trademark of and licensed by Universal City Studios, Inc.

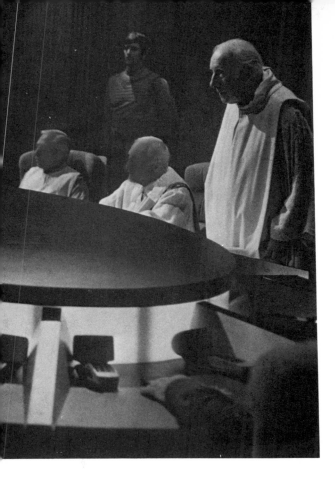

can public may not have agreed with his position as a conscientious objector, but people understood that Ayres was a fine actor, and that was what they went to the movies for. He returned to the screen in 1946 in *The Dark Mirror*, following that with excellent performances in *The Unfaithful* in 1947 and in *Johnny Belinda* in 1948, for which he received an Academy Award nomination for Best Actor.

In the years since, he has provided audiences with many memorable characterizations in such films as *Advise and Consent*, *The Carpetbaggers*, *The Man*, *Battle for the Planet of the Apes*, and *Earth II*.

His moment in "Battlestar Galactica" is brief, but memorable.

Wilfrid Hyde-White/*Anton*

Anton, a member of the Council of the Twelve, is a man who believes in reason and order. He is a pragmatist, the ultimate politician who seeks compromise, and only needs a rationalization to accept any point of view. He respects Adama, but he also wants to keep his associate, Sire Uri, satisfied. He is willing to accept Uri's plan to demobilize the Battlestar *Galactica* military force, but he feels it can be accomplished only if the people approve.

When Sire Uri reveals his plan to present his case at the ceremony honoring the three fliers, Anton smiles approvingly, "A brilliant suggestion, Uri. Just the tonic our people need at this moment. Some old-fashioned down-to-goodness heroes."

The urbane manners, the arch voice, the sense of gentle whimsy are unmistakable. They belong to English actor Wilfrid Hyde-White. He is such a delightful chameleon that the audience cannot hate him, even though he is obviously aiding and abetting the forces of evil.

He has delighted audiences in numerous films, from *The Third Man* in 1950 through *My Fair Lady* in 1964 to the films and television of today, having given outstanding performances in *The Golden Salamander*, *The Browning Version*, *Northwest Frontier*, *The Magic Christian*, *The Circle*, *The Liquidator*, and *P.J.*

Born the son of the Canon of Gloucester Cathedral, Wilfrid Hyde-White was schooled in England's scenic Cotswold Hills. At seventeen, he entered the Royal Academy of Dramatic Arts, where he was told he had no innate dramatic ability, but that he might achieve success by hard work and perseverance.

That estimation proved correct. He made his professional debut in the early 1920s in a touring company of *Tons of Money*, but he did not achieve success until eighteen years later in a revue, *Come Out of Your Shell*, which established a reputation for him on the London stage.

After many years in films, Wilfrid Hyde-White has chosen to divide his time among stage, television, and films. He recently toured Europe with co-star Douglas Fairbanks, Jr., in *The Pleasure of His Company*, and appeared on Broadway in the New York production of *The Jockey Club Stakes*.

THE IMPACT OF BATTLESTAR GALACTICA™*

At a price-tag of several million dollars for the first seven hours of film, "Battlestar Galactica" has turned out to be the most expensive series ever mounted for television. Through careful planning and effort, however, it has proved to have been worth every penny. Thirty to thirty-five million viewers every week have made its television ratings extremely high, and it seems set for a lengthy run.

The heroes, heroines, and villains of "Battlestar Galactica" are on their way to becoming a part of modern mythology. Eventu-

The Cylons™* attack the clones.

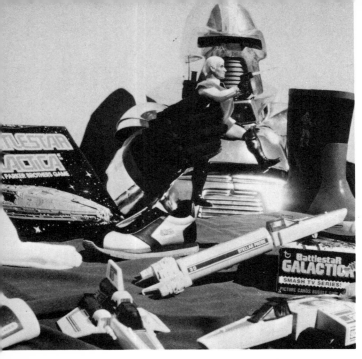

Here displayed are a few of the Battlestar Galactica™* items now or soon to be available on the market.

ally they may be to this generation what Captain Midnight, Buck Rogers, Superman, and Flash Gordon were to earlier generations.

"Battlestar Galactica" has all the makings of a never-ending saga of epic proportions, with heroes who are good and valorous, and with villains who represent genuine evils behind their incredible and unreal appearances. Good always triumphs over evil, yet the threat of evil never disappears completely.

The medium of television, of course, has made the creation of this epic saga greatly different from the creation of all of its predecessors. Although the overwhelming nature of its success was somewhat unexpected, it was planned and calculated for a degree of success from its inception in order to minimize the risk of its expensive production.

Created for ABC television by MCA-Universal Studios, the promotional aspects of "Battlestar Galactica" began over a year before the television premiere. The expected audience for the show was thus already familiar with some of its heroes, villains, and spacecraft before actually seeing them in action.

One of the most important parts of film and television promotion today is the licensing and merchandising of products related to the main product. Toys, games, wearing apparel, books are all means of making the public aware of a

*A trademark of and licensed by Universal City Studios, Inc.

film or show, while—at the same time—offering some financial return for a business that is often otherwise risky. The sales of these items are also an excellent gauge of the success of a show.

Steve Adler, vice-president in charge of merchandising, recalls, "We started our licensing program in the late spring of 1977, discussing licenses with Mattel for toy items. Monogram, which is a subsidiary company of Mattel, came out with model hobby kits as early as July of 1978, two months prior to the broadcast of the Battlestar Galactica television series, and they have sold well past their quota. They have advised us, as have several of our licensees, that 'Battlestar Galactica' items have been one of their most successful licenses."

Adler, who has been responsible for merchandising many of MCA-Universal's most successful films and shows, including "The Six Million Dollar Man," *Jaws*, *Jaws 2*, "Emergency," *The Wiz*, "The Bionic Woman," considers "Battlestar Galactica" his most successful licensing project. Many of the people in the MCA-Universal offices have commented that they have never seen so much enthusiasm from toy and game companies, manufacturers, and publishers.

"'Battlestar Galactica' is easily the most popular show that I've ever had to license," Adler tells. "It has been very gratifying, and I look forward to continued success with it."

Part of this success Adler attributes to the fact that the show has recognizable characters, identifiable mechanical devices, and a specific sense of style. "One of the most important aspects of any merchandising program is how visible the material from the show is on the products we license," Adler explains. "You really have to have something that will appeal to the imagination of the buying public. They are tempted by a variety of different products out there, and yours have to have something really unusual or exciting about them. They have to make a statement that the people buying can identify with. This is particularly true of wearing apparel; when a consumer buys a product, he is making a statement."

The Battlestar Galactica merchandise in the marketplace covers just about every aspect of modern life. Children especially can have almost anything they need, enjoy, or use associated in some way with the show—whether they want to identify with the heroes such as Apollo or Starbuck, or with villains such as the Cylons and the Ovions.

Toys and games are, of course, among the most popular items with children. Mattel toys and their subsidiary company, Monogram, manufacture action figures, electronic games, and hobby kits. They replicate the characters of the show in four-inch and nine-inch models. The Monogram kits include almost exact duplicates of the most important space ships in the show: the Colonial Vipers, the Cylon Raiders, and the Battlestar *Galactica*. Parker has licensed the games and puzzles, and a wide variety are already on the market, with more to come.

There is also Battlestar Galactica jewelery and Battlestar Galactica chewing gum with trading cards, through the Topps company; there

are wallpaper, a wall mural, and an assortment of posters. There are radios and amplifiers, stationery, and lunch kits. There are glasses and dishes, and there is a special kit for "Design Your Own" cups. General Mills offers Battlestar Galactica premiums with their cereal, and Wonder Bread with its bread. There are activity books, coloring books, sticker books comic books, novels, and photo-novels. There are sheets, pillowcases, towels, comforters, slumber bags, and draperies sold through the Bibb Company.

The list seems endless, and that doesn't include the wearing apparel, such as shirts, sneakers, pajamas, tank-tops, sweatshirts, rainwear, jackets, T-shirts, costumes, and masks. Audiences have so much admired the costumes created by Jean Pierre Dorleac for the show that plans are in the works to adapt the designs for sale through retail outlets, thereby making a great impact on fashion.

And this is only the beginning, for the early merchandising efforts were centered on the United States. Worldwide licensing did not

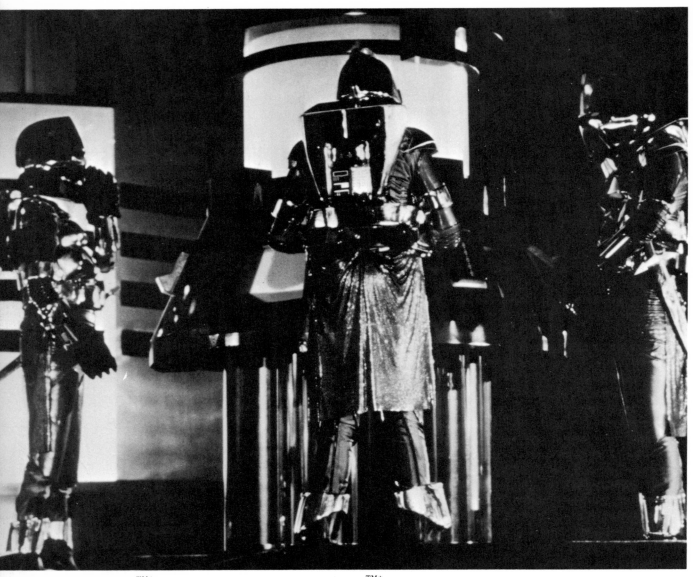

The Cylons™* aim the giant Pulsar cannon at Vipers™* entering the atmosphere of the Ice Planet.

begin until November of 1978, in preparation for the theatrical release of the motion picture *Battlestar Galactica* throughout the world, although, according to Adler, Battlestar Galactica fever hit London several months in advance.

Before the London opening, Adler revealed, "There is a lot of excitement over there about the posters and the T-shirts and the toys, even though the film will not be opening there until March or April of 1979. The excitement here in the United States has reached them, and they've heard about the high ratings and the extremely popular toys."

Although a relatively recent development in motion pictures and television, large-scale merchandising efforts will continue to affect the planning and producing of shows. Certainly, with "Battlestar Galactica" the economics are impressive. Although there were some fears associated with spending several million dollars for the first seven hours of television, before the show was even a few weeks old Adler's projection for the first year of merchandising alone was in the range of such millions of dollars as would pay for a large part of that investment.

"Battlestar Galactica products should sell on the retail market in an excess of $150,000,000 from the time it began on television on September 17, 1978 to September 17, 1979. That

*A trademark of and licensed by Universal City Studios, Inc.

translates roughly to $75,000,000 wholesale.

No matter what happens with the television series after the first year, "Battlestar Galactica" has to be considered a major success, both artistically and financially. It has become the show to beat on Sunday nights, and the other major networks will not be satisfied until they have thrown the best they have to offer up against it, hoping to win in the war of the ratings.

Adler, however, is confident that "Battlestar Galactica" will continue to win out over whatever forces are pitted against it. "I think 'Battlestar Galactica' will predominate and grow in strength. It is probably the most exciting new show on the air, and there's certainly

nothing in the family programming area to compare with it. The interesting thing about it is that it stretches the youngsters' imaginations; it brings all sorts of things, such as cloning, for example, into perspective for them. It does not make space such an unusual place; it shows the relevance between what could occur out in space and our everyday life; and it shows that there really is not much difference."

"Battlestar Galactica" is very much a part of our everyday lives now, bringing the real possibilities of space—and of space life—into our own homes. It is a major step in our popular culture; the children who grow up with the show are the children who may grow up to travel in space themselves.

Inside the Tombs of Kobol.

EPILOGUE

Fleeing from the Cylon tyranny, the last Battlestar, *Galactica*, leads a rag-tag fugitive fleet on a lonely quest—for a shining planet known as Earth.

A Colonial Landram™* and a Cylon™* fighter in a duel to the death.